Show me

MW01099154

Word for Windows 2.0
A Visual Guide to the Basics

Peter Aitken

File	Edit	View	Layout	Tools

New
Open
Retrieve
Close
Save
Run
Save As

File Manager

alpha
books

A Division of Prentice Hall Computer Publishing
11711 North College Avenue, Carmel, Indiana 46032 USA

International Standard Book Number: 1-56761-178-8
Library of Congress Catalog Card Number: 93-70255

95 94 93   8 7 6 5 4 3 2 1

Interpretation of the printing code: the rightmost number of the first series of numbers is the year of the book's printing; the rightmost number of the second series of numbers is the number of the book's printing. For example, a printing code of 93-1 shows that the first printing of the book occurred in 1993.

Screen reproductions in this book were created by means of the program Collage Plus from Inner Media, Inc., Hollis, NH.

Printed in the United States of America

TRADEMARKS

Publisher
Marie Butler-Knight

Associate Publisher
Lisa A. Bucki

Managing Editor
Elizabeth Keaffaber

Acquisitions Manager
Stephen R. Poland

Development Editor
Seta Frantz

Manuscript Editor
Audra Gable

Cover Designer
Scott Fullmer

Designer
Amy Peppler-Adams

Indexer
Jeanne Clark

Production Team
*Diana Bigham, Katy Bodenmiller, Scott Cook, Tim Cox,
Linda Koopman, Tom Loveman, Carrie Roth, Greg Simsic*

*Special thanks to C. Herbert Feltner for ensuring the
technical accuracy of this book.*

CONTENTS

INTRODUCTION

Have you ever said to yourself, "I wish someone would just *show me* how to use Word for Windows." If you have, this *Show Me* book is for you. In it, you won't find detailed explanations of what's going on in your computer each time you enter a command. Instead, you will see pictures that *show you*, step by step, how to perform a particular task.

This book will make you feel as though you have your very own personal trainer standing next to you, pointing at the screen and showing you exactly what to do.

WHAT IS MICROSOFT WORD FOR WINDOWS?

So what exactly is Word for Windows? It is a word processing program designed to be used for creating, editing, and printing documents. A *document* can be anything that contains words: a half-page memo, a 10-page report, or a 500-page book.

Most of the time, we'll just call the product Word rather than using the full name "Microsoft Word for Windows." Since Word is a Windows-based product, it's designed to be used from within another program, Microsoft Windows. If you're not familiar with Windows, don't worry—this book will ease you into it. (There is another version of Word, Word for DOS 5.5, that is not Windows-based, but we're not going to cover it in this book.)

If you haven't worked with a word processor in several years, be prepared for some big surprises. Word processors such as Word for Windows come with a huge assortment of features to dress up your documents. In addition to the basics of entering text, making corrections, and printing, you can:

- Change the letters and spacing to create professional-looking documents.

- Automatically check spelling and correct mistakes.

- Use headers, footers, footnotes, and page numbers, all automatically generated.

- Include pictures in your documents.

- Work on more than one document at the same time.

- Display information in tables.

- Preview and fine-tune your page before you print it.

What Does Word Look Like?

Word looks a lot like other Windows-based programs you may have seen. (If you haven't seen a Windows-based program before, that's okay.) The main screen is a rectangular window. The text you type appears in the middle, and around the edges are buttons, menus, borders, and other items that help you control Word.

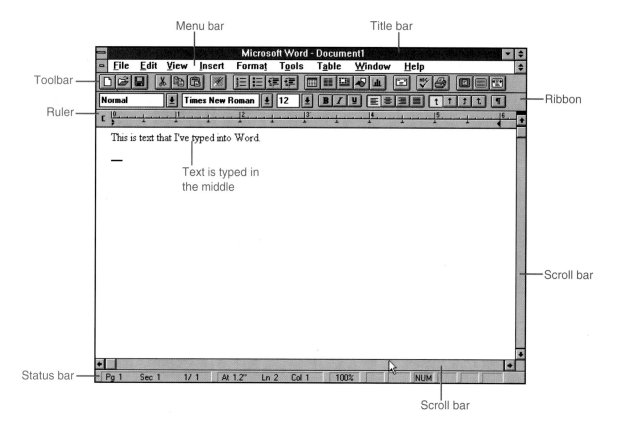

Don't worry about memorizing the parts of the window now; you'll learn more about them later in the book.

HOW TO USE THIS BOOK

Using this book is as simple as falling off your chair. Just flip to the task that you want to perform and follow the steps. You will see easy step-by-step instructions that tell you which keys to press and which commands to select. You will also see step-by-step pictures that show you what to do. Follow the steps or the pictures (or both) to complete the task. Here's an example of a set of instructions from this book.

Saving a Document for the First Time

1 Press **Alt+F** or click on File.

2 Press **A** or click on Save **As**.

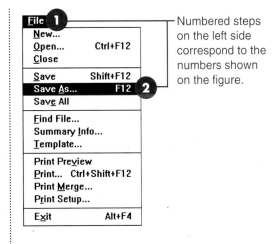

Numbered steps on the left side correspond to the numbers shown on the figure.

3 Enter the document name in the File Name box.

4 If desired, select drive, directory, and file type options.

5 Press **Enter** or click **OK**.

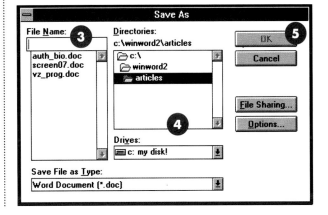

Every computer book has its own way of telling you which buttons to push and which keys to press. Here's how this book handles those formalities:

- Keys that you should press appear as they do on your keyboard (for example, press **Alt** or press **F10**). If you need to press more than one key at once, the keys are separated with plus signs. For example, if the text tells you to press **Alt+F**, hold down the **Alt** key while pressing the **F** key.

- Text that you should type is printed in **boldface type like this**.

- Some features are activated by selecting a menu and then a command. If I tell you to "select **F**ile **N**ew," you should open the **F**ile menu and select the **N**ew command. In this book, the selection letter is printed in boldface for easy recognition.

Definitions in Plain English

In addition to the basic step-by-step approach, pages may contain Learn the Lingo definitions to help you understand key terms. These definitions are placed off to the side, so you can easily skip them.

LEARNING THE LINGO

Pull-down menu: A menu that appears at the top of the screen, listing various commands. The menu is not visible until you select it from the menu bar. The menu then drops down, covering a small part of the screen.

Quick Refreshers

If you need to know how to perform some other task in order to perform the current task, look for a Quick Refresher. With the Quick Refresher, you won't have to flip through the book to learn how to perform the other task; the information is right where you need it.

QUICK REFRESHER

Making dialog box selections

Directories:
c:\

- c:\
- aol
- collage
- data
- dos
- execute
- fonts

Drives:
c: joe kraynak

File Name:
*.exe

☐ Run Minimized

New
○ Program Group
◉ Program Item

OK
Cancel

List box. Click on a list item to choose it. Use the scroll bar to view additional items.

Drop-down list. Click on the down arrow to the right of the list to display it. Click on the desired item.

Text box. Click to place the I-beam in the box. Type your entry.

Check box. Click on a box to select or deselect it. (You can select more than one.)

Option button. Click on a button to select it. (You can select only one button in a group.)

Command button. Click on a button to execute the command. (All dialog boxes have at least two command buttons: OK to execute your selections, and Cancel to cancel the selections.)

Tips, Ideas, and Shortcuts

Throughout this book, you will encounter tips that provide important information about a task or tell you how to perform the task more quickly.

TIP

Here are some keyboard shortcuts for working Word for Windows:

Open a document	CTRL + F12
Save a document	SHIFT + F12
Print a document	CTRL + SHIFT + F12
Cut	CTRL + X
Copy	CTRL + C
Paste	CTRL + V
Go To	F5
Exit Word	SHIFT + F4

Exercises

Because most people learn by doing, several exercises throughout the book give you additional practice performing a task.

Follow the following steps to make a directory at the DOS prompt, change to the directory, and delete it:

1 Type **cd** and press **Enter** to change to the root directory.

2 Type **md testdir** and press **Enter** to make the TESTDIR directory.

3 Type **cd\testdir** and press **Enter** to change to the TESTDIR directory.

4 Type **cd** and press **Enter** to change back to the root directory.

5 Type **rd testdir** and press **Enter** to remove the TESTDIR directory.

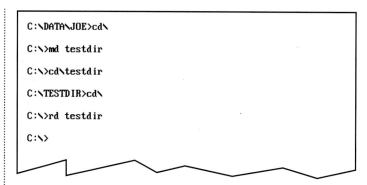

```
C:\DATA\JOE>cd\

C:\>md testdir

C:\>cd\testdir

C:\TESTDIR>cd\

C:\>rd testdir

C:\>
```

Where Should You Start?

If this is your first encounter with computers, read the next section, "Quick Computer Tour," before reading anything else. This section explains some computer basics that you need to know in order to get your computer up and running.

Once you know the basics, you can work through this book from beginning to end or skip around from task to task, as needed. If you decide to skip around, there are several ways you can find what you're looking for:

- Use the Table of Contents at the front of this book to find a specific task you want to perform.

- Use the complete index at the back of this book to look up a specific task or topic and find the page number on which it is covered.

- Use the color-coded sections to find groups of related tasks.

- Flip through the book and look at the task titles at the top of the pages. This method works best if you know the general location of the task in the book.

- Use the inside back cover of this book to quickly find the page on which a command you are looking for is covered.

QUICK COMPUTER TOUR

If this is your first time in front of a computer, the next few sections will teach you the least you need to know to get started.

Parts of a Computer

Think of a computer as a car. The system unit holds the engine that powers the computer. The monitor is like the windshield that lets you see where you're going. And the keyboard and mouse are like the steering wheel, which allow you to control the computer.

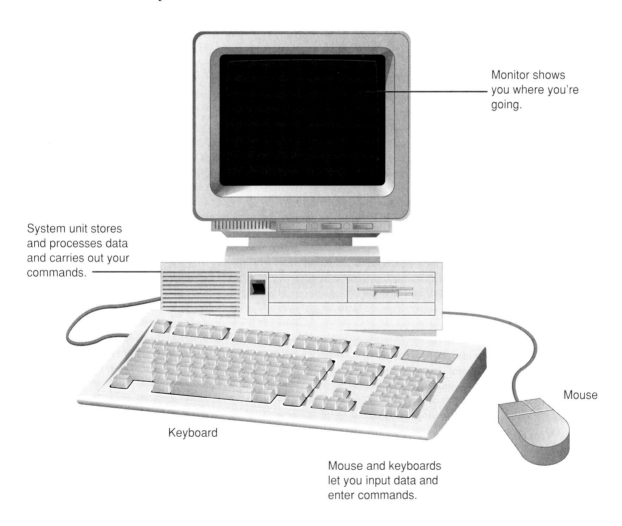

Monitor shows you where you're going.

System unit stores and processes data and carries out your commands.

Mouse

Keyboard

Mouse and keyboards let you input data and enter commands.

The System Unit

The system unit contains three basic elements: a central processing unit (CPU), which does all the "thinking" for the computer; random-access memory (RAM), which stores instructions and data while the CPU is processing it; and disk drives, which store information permanently on disks to keep the information safe. It also contains several ports (at the back), which allow you to connect other devices to it, such as a keyboard, mouse, and printer.

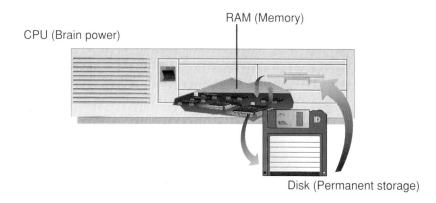

CPU (Brain power)

RAM (Memory)

Disk (Permanent storage)

Using a Keyboard

The keyboard is no mystery. It contains a set of alphanumeric (letter and number) keys for entering text, arrow keys for moving around on-screen, and function keys (F1, F2, and so on) for entering commands. It also has some odd keys, including Alt (Alternative), Ctrl (Control), and Esc (Escape) that perform special actions.

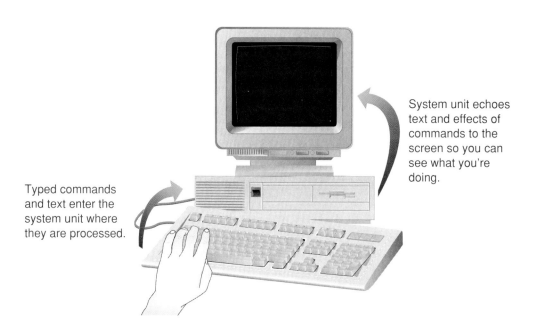

Typed commands and text enter the system unit where they are processed.

System unit echoes text and effects of commands to the screen so you can see what you're doing.

Using a Mouse

Like the keyboard, a mouse allows you to communicate with the computer. You roll the mouse around on your desk to move a *mouse pointer* on the screen. You can use the pointer to open menus and select other items on-screen. Here are some mouse techniques you must master:

Pointing. To point, roll the mouse on your desk until the tip of the mouse pointer is on the item to which you want to point.

Clicking. To click on an item, point to the desired item, and then hold the mouse steady while you press and release the mouse button. Use the left mouse button unless I tell you specifically to use the right button.

Double-clicking. To double-click, hold the mouse steady while you press and release the mouse button twice quickly.

Right-clicking. To right-click, click using the right mouse button instead of the left button.

Understanding Disks, Directories, and Files

Whatever you type (a letter, a list of names, a tax return) is stored only in your computer's temporary memory and is erased when the electricity is turned off. To protect your work, you must save it in a *file* on a *disk*.

A *file* is like a folder that you might use to store a report or a letter. You name the file, so you can later find and retrieve the information it contains.

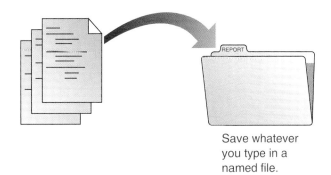

Save whatever you type in a named file.

Files are stored on *disks*. Your computer probably has a *hard disk* inside it (called drive C) to which you can save your files. You can also save files to *floppy disks*, which you insert into the slots (the floppy disk drives) on the front of the computer.

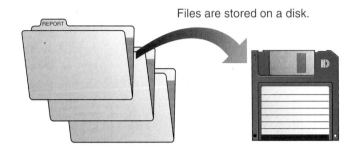

Files are stored on a disk.

To keep files organized on a disk, you can create *directories* on the disk. Each directory acts as a drawer in a filing cabinet, storing a group of related files. Although you can create directories on both floppy and hard disks, most people use directories only on hard disks.

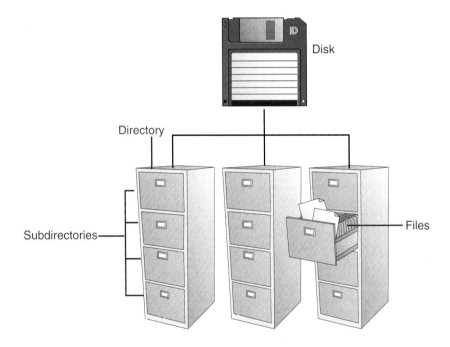

Disk

Directory

Subdirectories

Files

PART 1

Basic Word Tasks

Before you can run, you have to spend some time walking. In this section you will learn the most basic Word tasks—creating and saving a new document, typing text, and so on. Because so many of the more advanced features use these basic procedures as building blocks, you'll be glad later that you took the time to master them now.

- Starting Windows

- Starting Word

- The Word Screen

- Using Word Menus

- Working with Dialog Boxes

- Getting Help from Word

- Using the Word Help Index

- Exiting Word

STARTING WINDOWS

When to Start Windows

You must start Windows before you can use Word. Starting Windows displays the Windows desktop on your screen. You'll see the Program Manager, which you use to run other applications (such as Word).

Starting Windows

1 Turn on your computer and monitor.

2 At the DOS prompt, which looks like **C:>** or **C:\\>**, type **win** and press **Enter**.

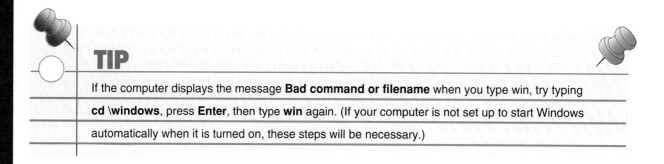

```
C:\>win 2
```

TIP

If the computer displays the message **Bad command or filename** when you type win, try typing

cd \\windows, press **Enter**, then type **win** again. (If your computer is not set up to start Windows

automatically when it is turned on, these steps will be necessary.)

When to Start Word

Before you can use Word to create or edit a document you must start, or run, it. This loads the program and displays it on your screen.

To start a program you use the Windows Program Manager screen, which is displayed when you start Windows. You need to locate the Word icon, a small graphical symbol with the label "Microsoft Word" below it.

The Microsoft Word for Windows icon

Program Manager

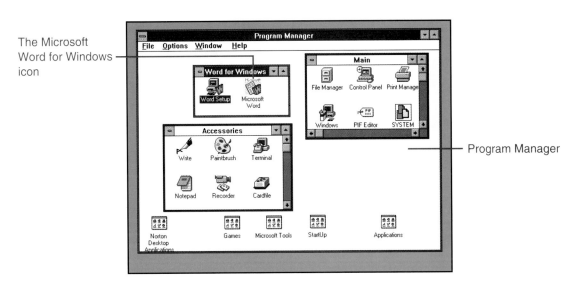

Starting Word

Follow these steps to start Word with the keyboard:

1 If the Word for Windows 2.0 program group is not open, press **Ctrl+Tab** until it is highlighted, and then press **Enter** to open it.

2 Press **Ctrl+Tab** until the Microsoft Word icon is highlighted.

3 Press **Enter**.

Basic Word Tasks

STARTING WORD

Or to start Word with the mouse, follow these steps:

1 If the Word for Windows 2.0 program group is not open, move your mouse until the mouse pointer (arrow) is positioned over the Word for Windows 2.0 program group icon.

2 If you performed step 1, quickly press and release the left mouse button twice (double-click) to open the program group.

3 Move your mouse until the mouse pointer (arrow) is positioned over the Microsoft Word icon.

4 Quickly press and release the left mouse button twice (double-click).

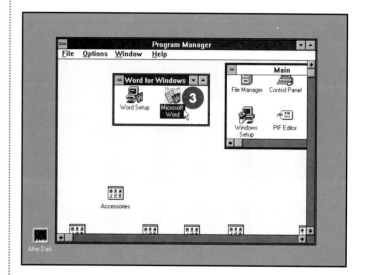

LEARNING THE LINGO

Icon: A small picture on the screen that represents a program, an action you can take, or a piece of information.

TIP

The icons displayed on your Program Manager screen depend on the programs that are installed on your computer. Your screens will probably not look exactly the same as the ones shown in this book.

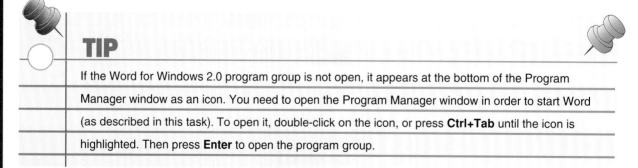

TIP

If the Word for Windows 2.0 program group is not open, it appears at the bottom of the Program Manager window as an icon. You need to open the Program Manager window in order to start Word (as described in this task). To open it, double-click on the icon, or press **Ctrl+Tab** until the icon is highlighted. Then press **Enter** to open the program group.

UNDERSTANDING THE WORD SCREEN

What Are the Parts of the Word Screen?

When you start Word, it displays the screen shown in the figure below. Each part of the screen has a name and a specific purpose.

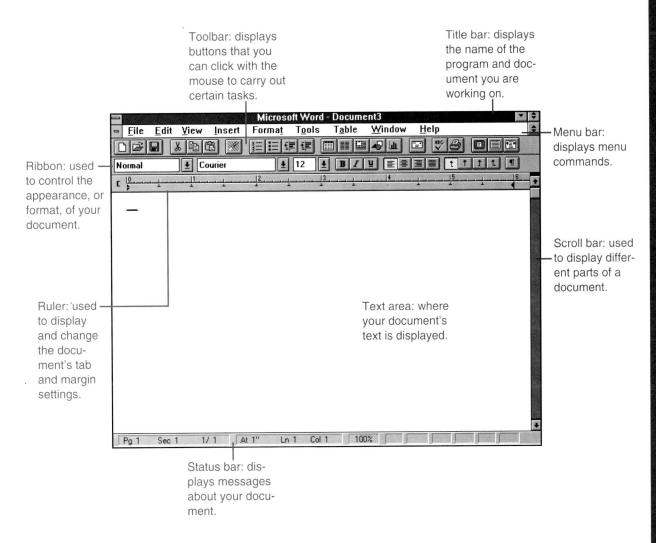

Toolbar: displays buttons that you can click with the mouse to carry out certain tasks.

Title bar: displays the name of the program and document you are working on.

Menu bar: displays menu commands.

Ribbon: used to control the appearance, or format, of your document.

Scroll bar: used to display different parts of a document.

Ruler: used to display and change the document's tab and margin settings.

Text area: where your document's text is displayed.

Status bar: displays messages about your document.

Basic Word Tasks

USING WORD MENUS

What Are Menus?

You use menus to issue commands to Word, telling it what you want it to do. To use Word menus and commands, you must first open the menu and then select the command of your choice. You can select menu commands using either the keyboard or the mouse.

All of Word's menus are listed on the menu bar on the second line of the Word screen.

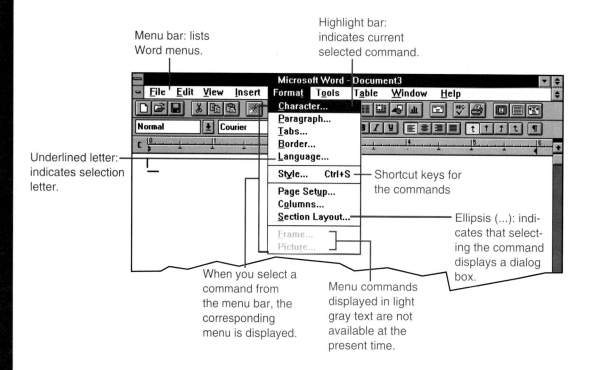

Menu bar: lists Word menus.

Highlight bar: indicates current selected command.

Underlined letter: indicates selection letter.

Shortcut keys for the commands

Ellipsis (...): indicates that selecting the command displays a dialog box.

When you select a command from the menu bar, the corresponding menu is displayed.

Menu commands displayed in light gray text are not available at the present time.

LEARNING THE LINGO

Shortcut key: A key, or combination of keys, you can use to issue a command without using the menus.

Ellipsis: Three dots (periods) following a menu command, which indicate that a dialog box will follow.

Selection letter: The underlined letter of the command or menu name. Keyboard users can select a command by typing the selection letter or can select a menu by holding down **Alt** and typing the selection letter.

Selecting Menu Commands

1 To select a command from the menu bar, press and hold **Alt**, and then press the key which corresponds to the underlined letter in the menu name. With the mouse, point and click on the menu name.

2 To select a command from the menu, press the key which corresponds to the underlined letter in the command. With the mouse, click on the command.

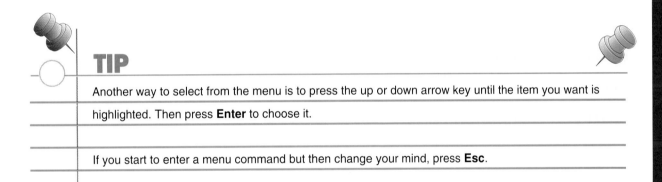

TIP

Another way to select from the menu is to press the up or down arrow key until the item you want is highlighted. Then press **Enter** to choose it.

If you start to enter a menu command but then change your mind, press **Esc**.

Basic Word Tasks

WORKING WITH DIALOG BOXES

What Is a Dialog Box?

A dialog box is a window that Word displays on-screen when it needs some information from you. A dialog box is often displayed when you enter a menu command. While every dialog box is different, they all share many common components. If you learn how to use these components, you'll be able to use any dialog box you encounter.

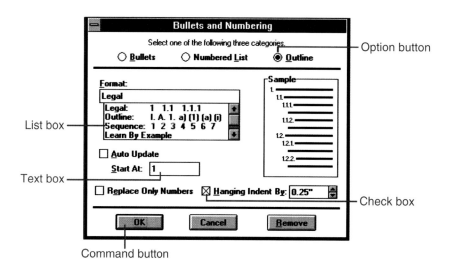

How to Use a Dialog Box

To select any item in a dialog box, click on it or press Alt plus the item's selection letter. Once the item is selected, use the item as noted in this table:

Dialog Box Elements

Fi**n**d What: ☐

Text box. Click or use the left and right arrow keys to position the vertical bar. Type an entry. Use Del and Backspace to erase, if necessary.

Dri**v**es:
🖬 c: my disk! ▼

List box. Double-click on the item you want.

Color:
■ Auto ▼

Drop-down list. Click on the down arrow to display the list. Click on the item you want.

File **N**ame:
☐
auth_bio.doc
screen07.doc
vz_prog.doc

Combo box. Enter and edit text in the box as you would in a text box, or click the desired item in the list.

Copies: 1 ▲▼

Number box. Enter a number in the box, or click the up and down arrows to increase or decrease the value.

☐ Match **W**hole Word Only

Check box. Click on the box to turn it on or off.

○ **U**p ● **D**own

Option button. Click on a button to turn it on and turn all others in the group off.

OK
Cancel

Command button. Click the button to execute or cancel the dialog box selections.

Basic Word Tasks

GETTING HELP FROM WORD

What Is Help?

Help is just what it sounds like—assistance with some task you are trying to perform. Word has a sophisticated Help system that can display information on-screen about any Word task.

Word's Help facility has several features that assist you in finding the information you need.

Displays the Help Table of Contents.

Shows a list of topics you have looked at already.

Searches for a particular Help topic.

Displays the next or previous Help topic.

Goes back to the last Help topic viewed.

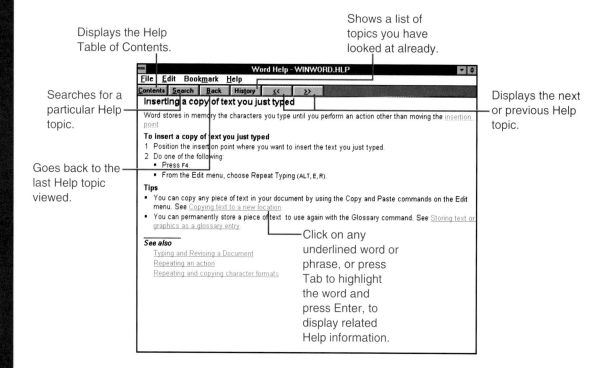

Click on any underlined word or phrase, or press Tab to highlight the word and press Enter, to display related Help information.

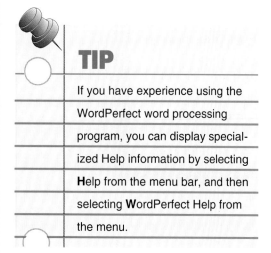

TIP

If you have experience using the WordPerfect word processing program, you can display specialized Help information by selecting **H**elp from the menu bar, and then selecting **W**ordPerfect Help from the menu.

TIP

See the task Using the Word Help Index to learn how to find any Help topic.

Press **F1** while any dialog box is displayed to see Help information about that dialog box.

To Get Help on a Menu Command

1 Display any menu by pressing **Alt** plus the underlined selection letter or by clicking on a menu command on the menu bar.

2 Use the up and down arrow keys to highlight the command on the menu.

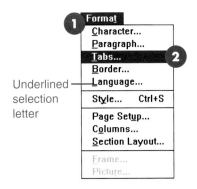

Underlined selection letter

3 Press **F1**.

4 When you're done viewing Help, press **Alt+F4** or click on **F**ile and E**x**it.

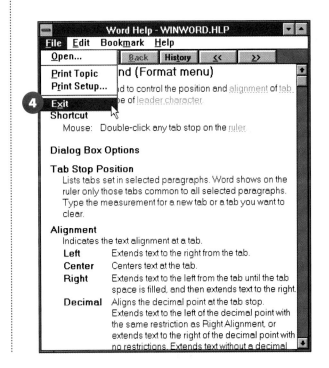

Basic Word Tasks

GETTING HELP FROM WORD

Exercise

Practice displaying Help information on menu commands.

1 Press **Alt+T** or click on Forma**t** to display the Format menu.

2 Press the down arrow once to highlight the **P**aragraph command.

3 Press **F1** to display Help information related to the Paragraph command.

4 Use the up and down arrow keys, PgUp, and PgDn, or use the scroll bar with the mouse to display different sections of the Help information.

5 Press **Alt+F4** or click on **F**ile and E**x**it to close Help.

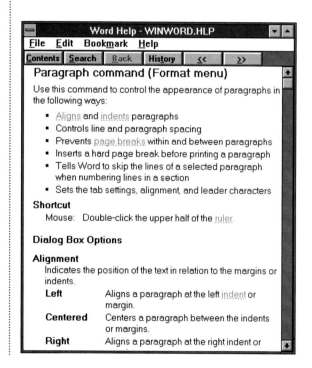

USING THE WORD HELP INDEX

What Is the Help Index?

Pressing F1 is fine if you know which menu or command you need to know about. But what if you want to set line spacing and you can't remember that it's controlled by the Format Paragraph command? In situations like this, the Help Index is handy.

The Help Index is like the index of a book. You can use it to find Help about any topic, even if you're not sure what the topic's official name is. To view the Help index, issue the **Help Index** command.

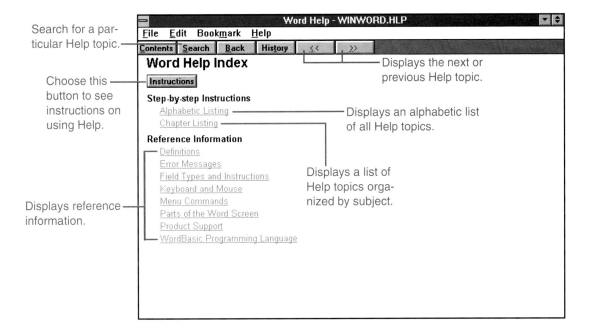

Search for a particular Help topic.

Choose this button to see instructions on using Help.

Displays reference information.

Displays the next or previous Help topic.

Displays an alphabetic list of all Help topics.

Displays a list of Help topics organized by subject.

TIP

At any time while you are viewing Help information, you can select the **C**ontents button to return to the Help index.

USING THE WORD HELP INDEX

Using the Help Index

1 Press **Alt+H** or click on **Help**.

2 Press **I** or click on Help Index.

3 Click on an underlined topic to view related information.

4 Click the **C**ontents button at any time to return to the Help index.

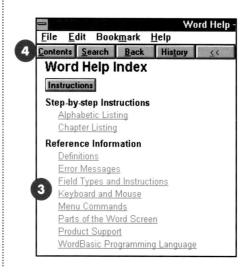

5 Press **Alt+F4** or click on **F**ile and E**x**it to close Help.

Exercise

Use the Help index to view the available Help information topics.

1 Select **Help** on the menu bar.

2 Select Help **I**ndex to display the Help index.

3 Click on **Alphabetic Listing** to display a listing of topics.

4 Use the PgUp and PgDn keys or the scroll bar to scroll through the list of topics.

5 Click on a topic.

6 If you have subtopics, click on the one you want.

7 Press **Alt+F4** or click on **F**ile and E**x**it to close Help.

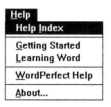

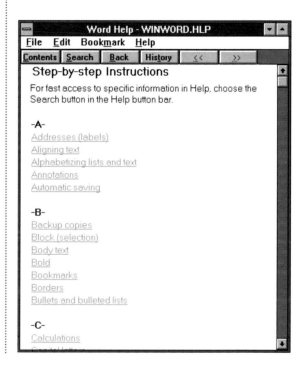

Basic Word Tasks

EXITING WORD

When Do You Exit Word?

When you're finished working in Word, you should exit the program. This frees up the system resources that Word is using so that you can run a different program.

Exiting Word

1 Press **Alt+F** or click on **File**.

2 Press **X** or click on **Exit**.

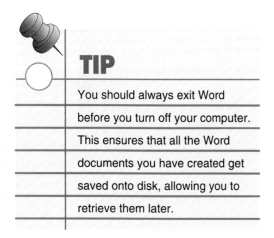

TIP

You should always exit Word

before you turn off your computer.

This ensures that all the Word

documents you have created get

saved onto disk, allowing you to

retrieve them later.

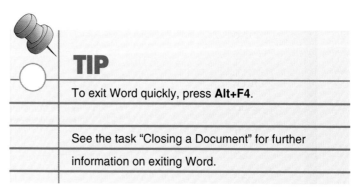

TIP

To exit Word quickly, press **Alt+F4**.

See the task "Closing a Document" for further

information on exiting Word.

PART 2

Creating, Editing, Saving, and Printing Documents

In this section you'll learn the basics of creating and editing documents. You'll also learn how to save your documents, how to open a document that you saved earlier, and how to print your documents.

- Entering Text
- Insert and Overstrike Modes
- Erasing Text
- Selecting Blocks of Text
- Text Selection Shortcuts
- Deleting Blocks of Text
- Using the Ruler
- Using the Toolbar
- Moving and Copying Text
- Searching for Text

- Replacing Text
- Saving a New Document
- Saving a Named Document
- Changing a Document's Name
- Opening a Document
- Printing an Entire Document
- Printing a Single Page
- Printing a Portion of a Document
- Closing a Document

ENTERING TEXT

Starting a Document

When you start Word you will see a blank document ready for you to enter text. You enter text just like you would using a typewriter. The main difference is that you don't have to press Enter at the end of each line, since Word automatically starts a new line when text reaches the right margin (this is called wrapping). You need to press Enter only when you want to start a new paragraph.

When you enter text, it appears on-screen at the location of the insertion point. The insertion point is marked by a blinking vertical line. The end of the document is marked by a short horizontal line.

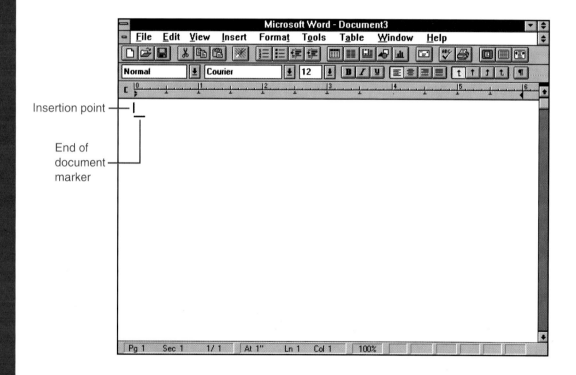

Insertion point

End of document marker

LEARNING THE LINGO

Document: The text that you are writing or editing—a letter, memo, report, and so on. No matter how many or how few characters, each group of text saved together in a file is a document.

Wrapping: Automatically starting a new line when you reach the right margin.

Insertion point: A short vertical line that marks the location where text you type will appear.

End of document marker: A short horizontal line that marks the end of the document.

You can move the insertion point by clicking in the new location. You can also move the insertion point using the keyboard.

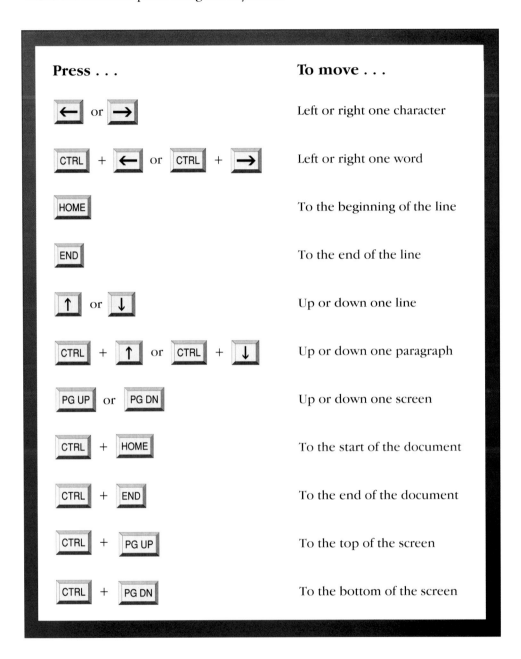

Press . . .	To move . . .
← or →	Left or right one character
CTRL + ← or CTRL + →	Left or right one word
HOME	To the beginning of the line
END	To the end of the line
↑ or ↓	Up or down one line
CTRL + ↑ or CTRL + ↓	Up or down one paragraph
PG UP or PG DN	Up or down one screen
CTRL + HOME	To the start of the document
CTRL + END	To the end of the document
CTRL + PG UP	To the top of the screen
CTRL + PG DN	To the bottom of the screen

Creating, Editing, Saving, and Printing Documents

ENTERING TEXT

Exercise

Enter the text shown in this figure and practice moving the insertion point and typing in additional text.

1 Type the date and press **Enter** three times.

2 Type **Dear Miss Jones:** and press **Enter** twice.

3 Type the two sentences of the letter, and then press **Enter** twice.

4 Type the closing, press **Enter** four times, and then type your name.

5 Position the insertion point immediately after the word "are" in the first sentence and type **all** followed by a space.

6 Position the insertion point immediately after the word "Monday" in the second sentence and type a comma.

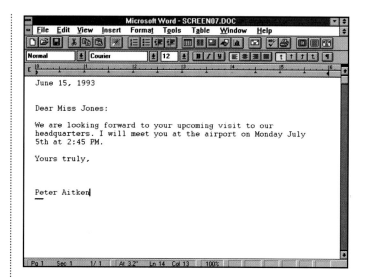

INSERT AND OVERSTRIKE MODES

When to Use Insert and Overstrike Mode

Word has two methods for entering text. In Insert mode, existing text moves over (to the right) to make room for the new text you're typing. In Overstrike mode, existing text is replaced (written over) by new text on a character-by-character basis (this is applicable only when there is text to the right of the insertion point).

Entering Text in Insert and Overstrike Modes

1 Position the insertion point where you want new text to appear by using the arrow keys or clicking.

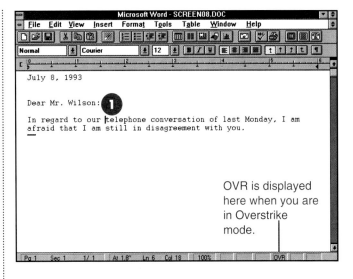

OVR is displayed here when you are in Overstrike mode.

2 Press the **Ins** key to switch between Insert and Overstrike modes.

31

INSERT AND OVERSTRIKE MODES

Exercise

Enter the text shown in this figure and practice typing in text in both Insert and Overstrike modes.

1 Type in the letter as shown in the figure.

2 Move the insertion point to the left of the word "Monday."

3 Press **Ins** to switch to Overstrike mode. Verify that OVR is displayed in the status bar.

4 Type **Tuesda**.

5 Press **Ins** to switch back to Insert mode. Verify that OVR is not displayed in the status bar.

6 Type **y**.

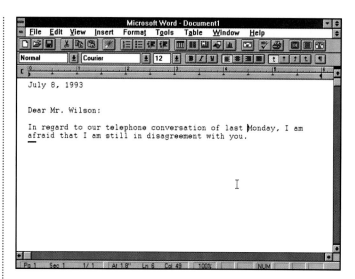

ERASING TEXT

Why Erase Text?

Everyone makes mistakes that need to be corrected. With Word you can throw away your white-out! You can easily erase, or delete, text one character at a time.

BACKSPACE — This key erases the character to the left of the insertion point

DELETE — This key erases the character to the right of the insertion point

QUICK REFRESHER

← or →	Moves left or right one character.
HOME	Moves to the beginning of the line.
END	Moves to the end of the line.
↑ or ↓	Moves up or down one line.
PG UP or PG DN	Moves up or down one screen.
CTRL + HOME	Moves to the start of the document.
CTRL + END	Moves to the end of the document.

TIP

See the task "Deleting Blocks of Text" to learn how to delete large amounts of text quickly.

TIP

If you press and hold either **Del** or **Backspace**, it will automatically repeat. Be careful—it's easy to delete more characters than you mean to!

ERASING TEXT

Erasing Text

1 Move the insertion point to the character to be deleted.

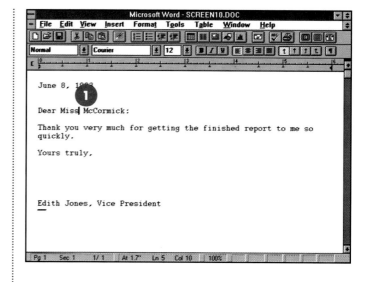

2 Press **Del** to delete the character to the right of the insertion point or press **Backspace** to delete the character to the left of the insertion point.

Exercise

Enter the text shown in this figure and then make the following corrections:
change "Miss" to "Ms.," and change "Yours truly" to "Sincerely yours."

1 Enter the text as shown in the figure.

2 Move the insertion point to the greeting, just to the right of the word "Miss."

3 Press **Backspace** four times.

4 Type **Ms.**

5 Move the insertion point to the beginning of the line that says "Yours truly,".

6 Press **Del** 11 times.

7 Type **Sincerely yours**.

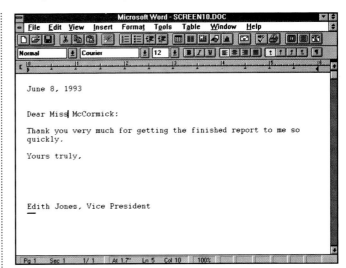

Creating, Editing, Saving, and Printing Documents

SELECTING BLOCKS OF TEXT

Why Select Text?

Selecting text is a necessary step in many of the editing procedures that you'll use. You select text to tell Word what part of the document to act on. Text that has been selected is highlighted, or displayed as white letters on a black background. In this figure, the second sentence is selected.

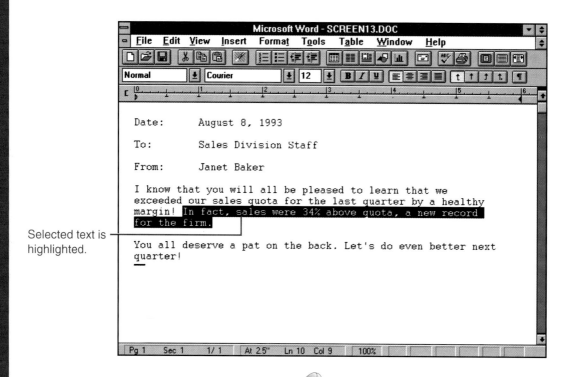

Selected text is highlighted.

LEARNING THE LINGO

Highlighted text: Text that has been selected for some action. It appears with the colors "reversed" to show that it is specially marked.

TIP

When you select text, its colors reverse—black-on-white becomes white-on-black. If you change the color of your document's on-screen background to something other than white, selected text will appear as the opposite color from the background. For example, if you have black text on a yellow window background, highlighted text will show up as white text with a blue background.

Selecting Text with the Mouse

1 Move the mouse until the I-beam is positioned at the beginning of the text that you want to select.

2 Press the left mouse button and hold it down.

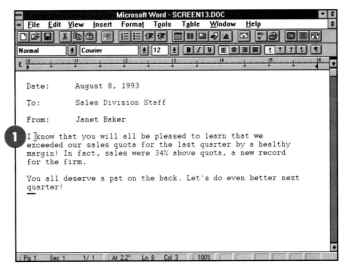

3 Move the mouse until the I-beam is positioned at the end of the text you want to select. The highlighted area will expand as you move the mouse.

4 Release the mouse button.

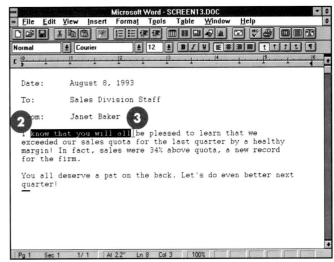

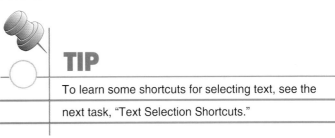

TIP

To learn some shortcuts for selecting text, see the next task, "Text Selection Shortcuts."

37

Creating, Editing, Saving, and Printing Documents

SELECTING BLOCKS OF TEXT

Selecting Text with the Keyboard

1 Move the insertion point to the beginning of the text.

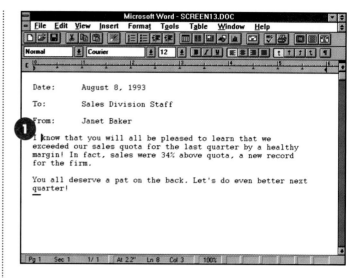

2 Press and hold the **Shift** key.

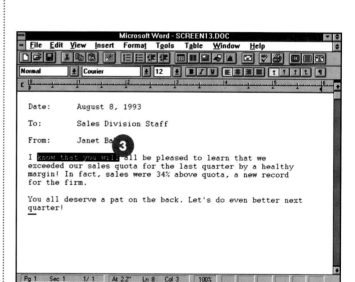

3 Move the insertion point to the end of the text you want to select.

4 Release the Shift key.

Exercise

Enter the text shown in the figure and practice selecting blocks of text.

1 Move the insertion point to the start of the second line, just before "exceeded."

2 Press and hold **Shift**.

3 Press the right arrow key until the highlight expands to the end of the word "quota."

4 Release Shift, and then press the left arrow key to cancel the selection.

5 Move the mouse until the I-beam is positioned at the start of the word "sales" in the second sentence.

6 Press and hold the left mouse button.

7 Move the mouse to expand the highlight to the end of the line, and then release the mouse button.

8 Click anywhere on the text to cancel the selection.

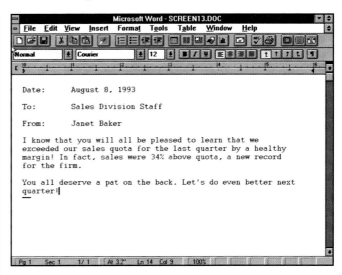

Microsoft Word - SCREEN13.DOC

File Edit View Insert Format Tools Table Window Help

Normal   Courier   12

```
Date:      August 8, 1993

To:        Sales Division Staff

From:      Janet Baker

I know that you will all be pleased to learn that we
exceeded our sales quota for the last quarter by a healthy
margin! In fact, sales were 34% above quota, a new record
for the firm.

You all deserve a pat on the back. Let's do even better next
quarter!
```

Pg 1   Sec 1   1/ 1   At 3.2"   Ln 14   Col 9   100%

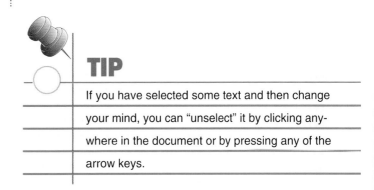

TIP

If you have selected some text and then change your mind, you can "unselect" it by clicking anywhere in the document or by pressing any of the arrow keys.

Creating, Editing, Saving, and Printing Documents

TEXT SELECTION SHORTCUTS

Why Use Shortcuts?

As you work on your documents, you'll find yourself selecting text a lot. Using these shortcuts can save you a lot of time and effort.

Some of these techniques use the mouse and the selection bar. This is the area of the screen just to the left of the text. You can tell when the mouse pointer is in the selection bar because it changes from an I-beam to an arrow.

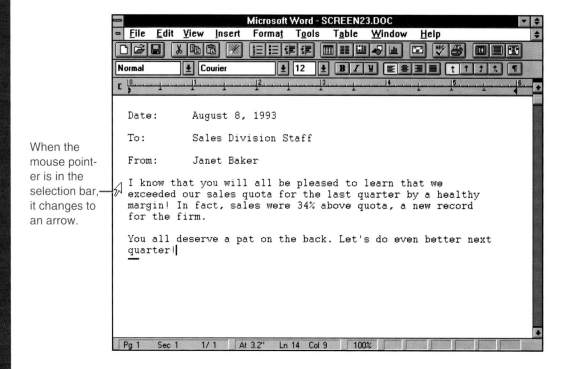

When the mouse pointer is in the selection bar, it changes to an arrow.

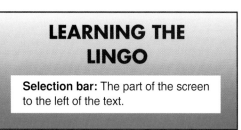

LEARNING THE LINGO

Selection bar: The part of the screen to the left of the text.

How to Use Text Selection Shortcuts

Double-click to select a word.

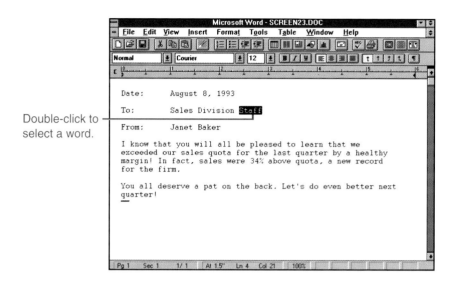

Press Ctrl and click to select a sentence.

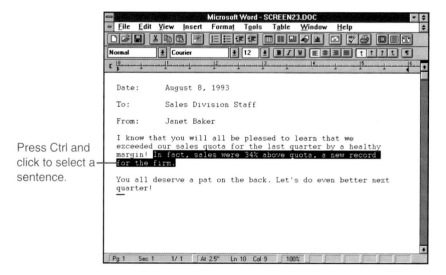

QUICK REFRESHER

Here's a brief reminder of some important mouse actions:

Point: To move the mouse so that the on-screen mouse pointer touches the desired item.

Click: To press and release the left mouse button.

Double-click: To press and release the left mouse button twice quickly.

Drag: To hold down the left mouse button while moving the mouse.

TEXT SELECTION SHORTCUTS

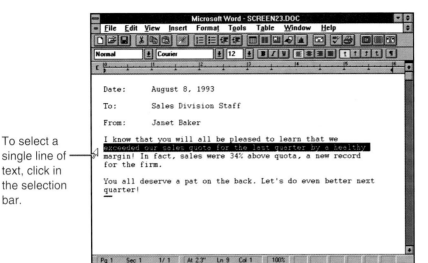

To select a single line of text, click in the selection bar.

To select multiple lines of text, point at the first line in the selection bar and press the left mouse button.

Drag to the last line and release the mouse button.

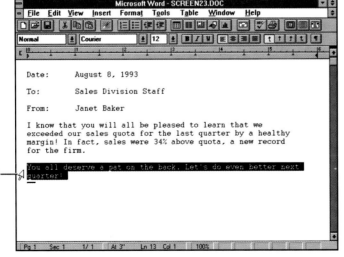

To select one paragraph, double-click in the selection bar.

Exercise

Enter the text shown in this figure and practice selecting different sections of the text.

1 Select the word **report** in the first sentence by double-clicking on it.

2 Select the first sentence in the second paragraph by clicking on it while holding the **Ctrl** key.

3 Select the entire first paragraph by double-clicking in the selection bar.

4 Select the last line in the second paragraph by clicking in the selection bar.

5 Select the second and third lines in the first paragraph by clicking and dragging in the selection bar.

6 Select the entire document by pressing **Ctrl+5** (on the numeric keypad).

TIP

To select the entire document press and hold the **Ctrl** key, and then press **5** on the numeric keypad on the right side of your keyboard. (If this doesn't work, try pressing the **NumLock** key once, and then try the 5 again.)

Creating, Editing, Saving, and Printing Documents

DELETING BLOCKS OF TEXT

How to Delete Blocks of Text

If you need to delete a large amount of text, it is easiest to delete it as a block rather than one character at a time. You can delete any size block of text from a single character to an entire document.

Deleting a Block of Text

1 Use the mouse or the keyboard to select the text that you want deleted.

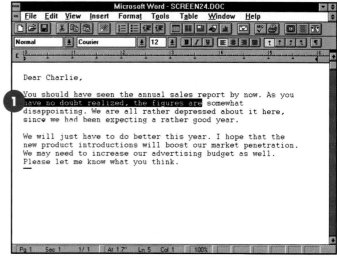

2 Press **Del**.

Exercise

Enter the text shown in the figure and practice deleting blocks of text.

1 Select the word **should** in the first sentence by double-clicking it.

2 Press **Del**.

3 Select the word **somewhat** in the second sentence by double-clicking on it.

4 Type **very**.

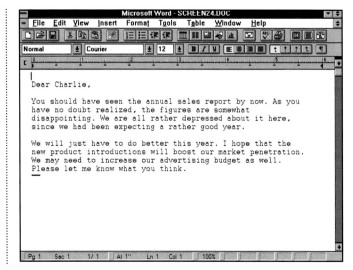

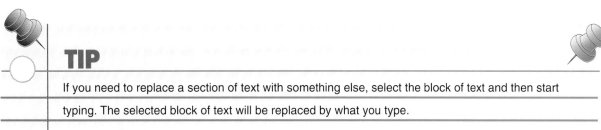

TIP

If you need to replace a section of text with something else, select the block of text and then start typing. The selected block of text will be replaced by what you type.

Creating, Editing, Saving, and Printing Documents

USING THE RULER

What Is the Ruler?

The Ruler is displayed on your screen directly above the document area. The Ruler shows current settings of tabs, indents, and margins and can be used to quickly change these settings. If the Ruler is not visible, issue the **View Ruler** command to display it.

The Ruler can display one of two scales. The Indent scale is used for indents and tabs.

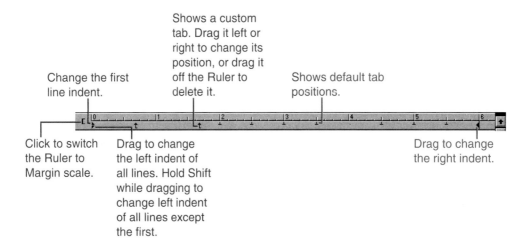

Shows a custom tab. Drag it left or right to change its position, or drag it off the Ruler to delete it.

Shows default tab positions.

Change the first line indent.

Click to switch the Ruler to Margin scale.

Drag to change the left indent of all lines. Hold Shift while dragging to change left indent of all lines except the first.

Drag to change the right indent.

The Margin scale is used for setting margins.

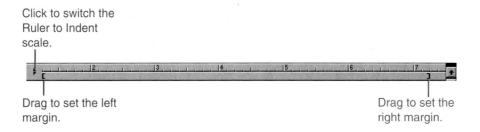

Click to switch the Ruler to Indent scale.

Drag to set the left margin.

Drag to set the right margin.

Using the Ruler

1 Select the paragraphs whose settings you want to change, or move the insertion point to the location where you want the new settings to take effect.

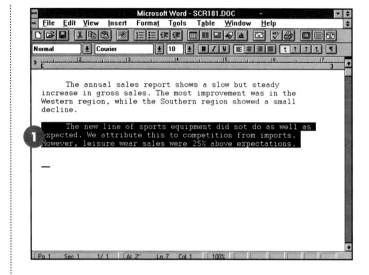

2 Click to switch to Indent scale.

3 Drag to change the left indent.

4 Drag to change the right indent.

5 Drag to change or delete custom tab stops.

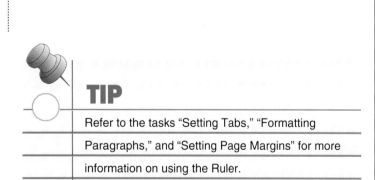

TIP

Refer to the tasks "Setting Tabs," "Formatting Paragraphs," and "Setting Page Margins" for more information on using the Ruler.

Creating, Editing, Saving, and Printing Documents

USING THE TOOLBAR

What Is the Toolbar?

The Toolbar is displayed on your screen directly below the menu bar. It contains a number of icons, or small graphical images, that represent frequently needed Word commands or tasks. To carry out a task or command, simply click the corresponding Toolbar icon.

If the Toolbar is not visible on your screen, issue the **View T**oolbar command to display it.

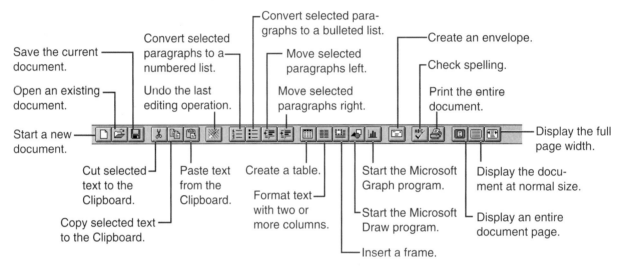

Save the current document.

Open an existing document.

Start a new document.

Convert selected paragraphs to a numbered list.

Undo the last editing operation.

Convert selected paragraphs to a bulleted list.

Move selected paragraphs left.

Move selected paragraphs right.

Create an envelope.

Check spelling.

Print the entire document.

Display the full page width.

Cut selected text to the Clipboard.

Copy selected text to the Clipboard.

Paste text from the Clipboard.

Create a table.

Format text with two or more columns.

Start the Microsoft Graph program.

Start the Microsoft Draw program.

Insert a frame.

Display the document at normal size.

Display an entire document page.

TIP

Some of the Toolbar icons represent commands or tasks that are not covered in this book. Please refer to the Word Help system or documentation for more information.

Using the Toolbar to Cut and Paste Text

1 Select the text to be cut.

2 Click on the **Cut** tool on the Toolbar.

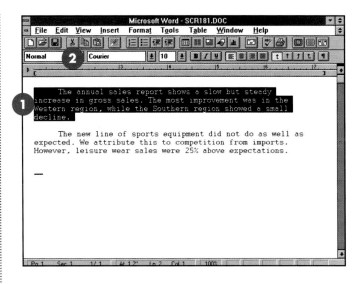

3 Move the insertion point to the new location for the text.

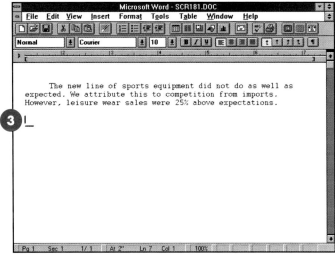

4 Click on the **Paste** tool on the Toolbar.

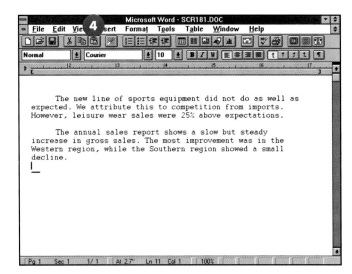

Creating, Editing, Saving, and Printing Documents

MOVING AND COPYING TEXT

Why Move or Copy Text?

You'll find that much of your editing time is spent polishing and rearranging documents. Word's ability to quickly copy or move sections of text from one location to another can be a real time-saver.

Like most Windows-based programs, Word uses the Clipboard to cut, copy, and paste. You copy or cut text or graphics from your document, and then reposition the cursor and paste the item at the new location. When you move text, you use Cut to remove the text from the old location and then Paste to insert it at the new location. When you copy text, you use Copy to copy the text from its original location and then Paste to insert the copy somewhere else.

Moving and Copying Text

1 Select the text using the mouse or keyboard.

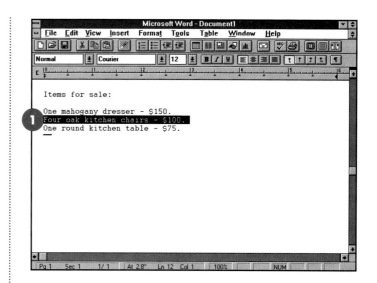

2 Press **Alt+E** or click on **Edit**.

3 To copy the text, press **C** or click on **Copy**. To move the text, press **T** or click on **Cut**.

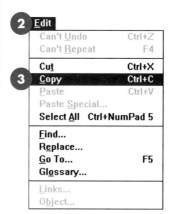

4 Move the insertion point to the location where you want the text placed.

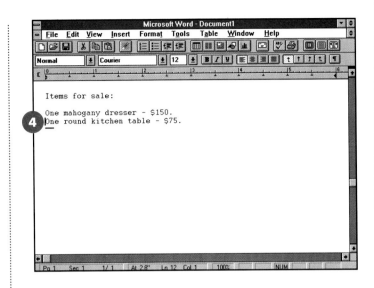

5 Press **Alt+E** or click on Edit.

6 Press **P** or click on **P**aste.

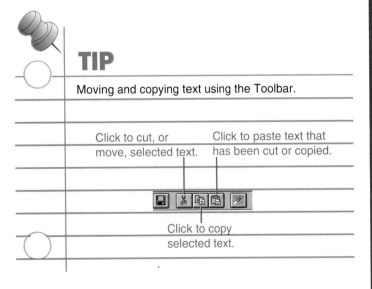

TIP

Here's a quicker way to move or copy text: After selecting the text, press **Ctrl+C** to copy it to the Clipboard or **Ctrl+X** to cut it to the Clipboard. Then move the insertion point to the new location and press **Ctrl+V** to paste it into the document.

TIP

Moving and copying text using the Toolbar.

Click to cut, or move, selected text.

Click to paste text that has been cut or copied.

Click to copy selected text.

Creating, Editing, Saving, and Printing Documents

MOVING AND COPYING TEXT

Exercise

Enter the text shown in the figure and practice moving and copying text.

1 Select the entire line that lists the mahogany dresser.

2 Issue the **Edit Cut** command.

3 Move the insertion point to the end of the document.

4 Issue the **Edit Paste** command.

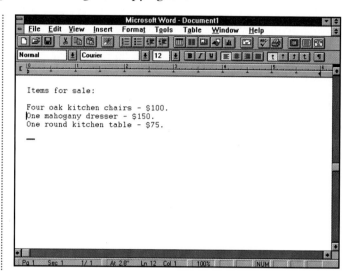

LEARNING THE LINGO

Clipboard: A temporary storage area built into most Windows-based programs. You can put a selection into the Clipboard with the Cut or Copy commands, and retrieve a selection from the Clipboard with the Paste command.

Copy: To duplicate a section of text and insert it in a new location. You end up with two copies of the text, one in the original location and one in the new location.

Move: To move a section of text from one location to another. You end up with one copy of the text in the new location.

QUICK REFRESHER

To select text with the keyboard

1 Move the insertion point to the start of the text.

2 Press and hold **Shift**.

3 Move the insertion point to the end of the text.

4 Release the Shift key.

To select text with the mouse

1 Move the I-beam to the start of the text.

2 Press and hold the mouse button.

3 Drag the highlight to the end of the text.

4 Release the mouse button.

Why Search for Text?

Searching for text lets you locate any word or phrase in your document. For example, if you are writing a novel and can't remember whether you introduced the character Henri in Chapter 2, you could search Chapter 2 for "Henri."

You use the **Edit Find** command to search for text. Issuing this command displays the Find dialog box.

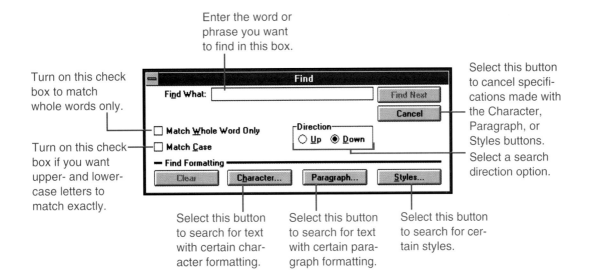

Enter the word or phrase you want to find in this box.

Turn on this check box to match whole words only.

Turn on this check box if you want upper- and lower-case letters to match exactly.

Select this button to cancel specifications made with the Character, Paragraph, or Styles buttons.

Select a search direction option.

Select this button to search for text with certain character formatting.

Select this button to search for text with certain paragraph formatting.

Select this button to search for certain styles.

LEARNING THE LINGO

Whole Words Only: Only whole words will be found. For example, if you are searching for "and" Word will not consider "band" to be a match.

Match Case: Word matches upper- and lowercase letters. For example, "Sales" will not match "sales" or "SALES."

Direction: Up searches backwards from the insertion point, and Down searches forwards from the insertion point.

SEARCHING FOR TEXT

Searching for Text

1 Press **Alt+E** or click on **Edit**.

2 Press **F** or click on **Find**.

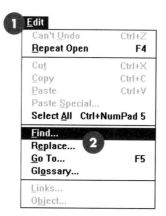

3 Enter the word or phrase you want to find in the Find What box.

4 Select the desired matching and direction options.

5 Click **Find** Next or press **Enter** to start the search.

6 Word highlights the first occurrence of the text. Click **Find** Next or press **Enter** to find the next occurrence.

7 Click on **Cancel** or press **Esc** to close the dialog box and return to editing the document.

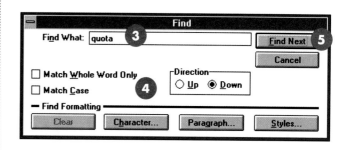

Word finds "quota" in the text.

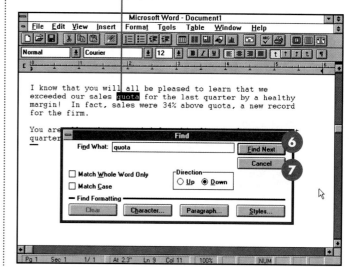

Exercise

Enter the text shown in the figure. Practice using the **Edit Find** command to locate specific text.

1 Move the insertion point to the start of the document.

2 Issue the **Edit Find** command.

3 Type **quota** in the Find What box.

4 Click Find Next or press **Enter**.

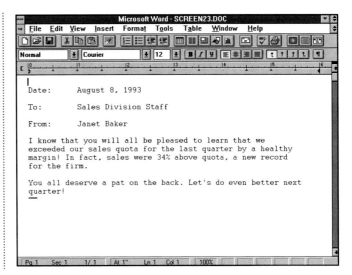

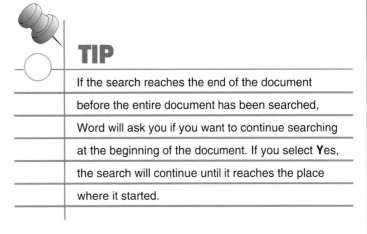

TIP

If Word cannot find the text, it displays the message **The search text is not found.** If you feel sure that the text is in the document, check the spelling of the text you entered in the Find What box and the setting of the Match Whole Word Only and Match Case options.

TIP

If the search reaches the end of the document before the entire document has been searched, Word will ask you if you want to continue searching at the beginning of the document. If you select **Y**es, the search will continue until it reaches the place where it started.

Creating, Editing, Saving, and Printing Documents

REPLACING TEXT

Why Replace Text?

When you are editing a document you will often need to change text from one thing to another. If you know the text that needs to be changed, you can have Word find and replace it automatically.

To replace text, issue the Edit Replace command to display the Replace dialog box.

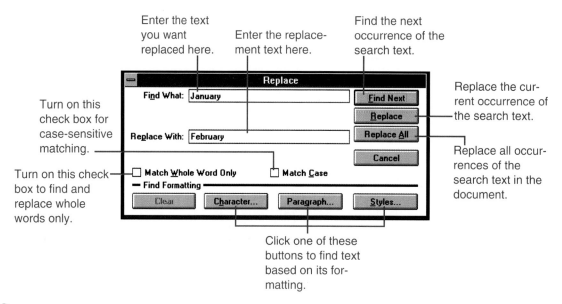

Enter the text you want replaced here.

Enter the replacement text here.

Find the next occurrence of the search text.

Turn on this check box for case-sensitive matching.

Replace the current occurrence of the search text.

Turn on this check box to find and replace whole words only.

Replace all occurrences of the search text in the document.

Click one of these buttons to find text based on its formatting.

TIP

To delete all occurrences of the specified text in your document, use the Edit Replace command but leave the Replace With box empty.

To Find and Replace Text

1 Press **Alt+E** or click **E**dit.

2 Press **E** or click **R**eplace.

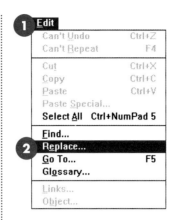

3 Enter the text you want to replace.

4 Enter the replacement text.

5 Select options for whole word or case matching.

6 Click a button to replace one or all occurrences of the text.

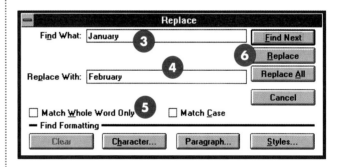

57

Creating, Editing, Saving, and Printing Documents

SAVING A NEW DOCUMENT

Why Save Your Document?

Saving your document will enable you to open the document the next time you use Word and to continue working right where you left off. While you are editing a document, it is kept in the computer's memory, a storage area that "forgets" everything when the computer is turned off. When you save a document it is stored on the computer's disk, which does not forget.

When you save a document for the first time you will need to assign a file name to identify it. The file name must be 1-8 characters long and can contain letters, numbers, and the underscore character (_); it cannot contain any spaces. Most file names have two parts: the file name itself, and the extension. The two parts are separated by a period.

You use the **File Save As** command to save your document for the first time. This command displays the Save As dialog box.

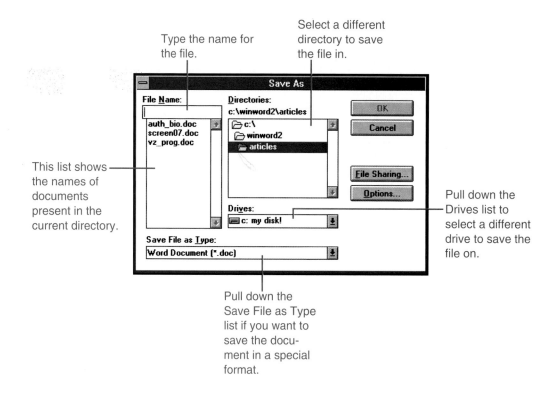

Type the name for the file.

Select a different directory to save the file in.

This list shows the names of documents present in the current directory.

Pull down the Drives list to select a different drive to save the file on.

Pull down the Save File as Type list if you want to save the document in a special format.

Saving a Document for the First Time

1 Press **Alt+F** or click on File.

2 Press **A** or click on Save **As**.

3 Enter the document name in the File **N**ame box.

4 If desired, select drive, directory, and file type options.

5 Press **Enter** or click **OK**.

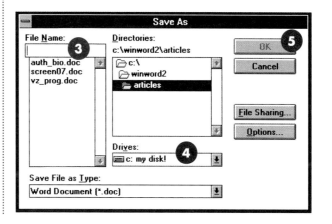

File
New...
Open...   Ctrl+F12
Close
Save   Shift+F12
Save As...   F12
Save All
Find File...
Summary Info...
Template...
Print Preview
Print...   Ctrl+Shift+F12
Print Merge...
Print Setup...
Exit   Alt+F4
1 SCREENS.DOC
2 SHOWWFW1.DOC
3 SCREEN23.DOC
4 SCREEN27.DOC

Save As
File Name: / auth_bio.doc / screen07.doc / vz_prog.doc
Directories: c:\winword2\articles
Drives: c: my disk!
Save File as Type: Word Document (*.doc)

TIP

Give each document a name that will help identify its contents. For example, a letter to George Smith could be called LTR_GS, and the first quarter sales report might be called SALES_Q1.

LEARNING THE LINGO

File name: A name assigned to a document stored on disk. You choose the first part of the name, up to 8 characters long. Word automatically adds the extension .DOC at the end of the file name.

Creating, Editing, Saving, and Printing Documents

SAVING A NEW DOCUMENT

Exercise

Enter the text shown in the figure and save it with the name SAMPLE1.

1 Press **Alt+F** or click **F**ile.

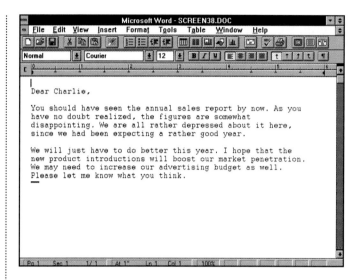

2 Press **A** or click Save **A**s.

3 Type **SAMPLE1**.

4 Press **Enter** or click **OK**.

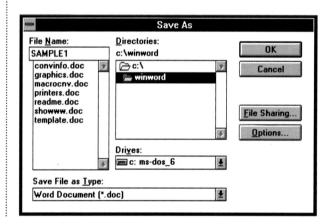

TIP

The document name is displayed in the title bar at the top of the screen. If the document has not been saved yet, the title bar reads Document1, Document2, and so on.

60

SAVING A NAMED DOCUMENT

Why Save Your Document?

You must save your document if you want to work on it again some other time. Even after you have saved a document once and given it a name, you must continue to save it as you work on it. This way, the changes you make will be saved.

How to Save a Document

1 Press **Alt+F** or click on File.

2 Press **S** or click on Save.

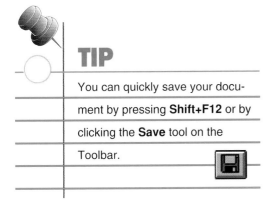

1 File
New...
Open...   Ctrl+F12
Close

Save   Shift+F12
2 Save As...   F12
Save All

Find File...
Summary Info...
Template...

Print Preview
Print... Ctrl+Shift+F12
Print Merge...
Print Setup...

Exit   Alt+F4

1 SCREEN38.DOC
2 SCREEN24.DOC
3 SCREENS.DOC
4 SHOWWFW1.DOC

TIP

You can quickly save your document by pressing **Shift+F12** or by clicking the **Save** tool on the Toolbar.

TIP

If you issue the **F**ile **S**ave command before your document has been named, Word will display the Save As dialog box. You can then enter a name for the file as explained in the task "Saving a New Document."

Creating, Editing, Saving, and Printing Documents

SAVING A FILE WITH A DIFFERENT NAME

Why Save with a Different Name?

Saving a file with a different name can come in handy. You might want to save a file under a different name for several reasons, such as:

- You want to make changes to it, but retain the original version too.

- You want to save the file to a different location, but retain the copy in the original location.

For example, let's say you have a file called PRELIM.DOC that lists your preliminary notes. After you've opened and modified it, you may want to save the document under a different name, such as FINAL.DOC. No problem. Word saves the document as FINAL.DOC and keeps PRELIM.DOC around in its original form in case you ever need to refer to it again.

To save the document with a new name, issue the **File Save As** command. This displays the Save As dialog box.

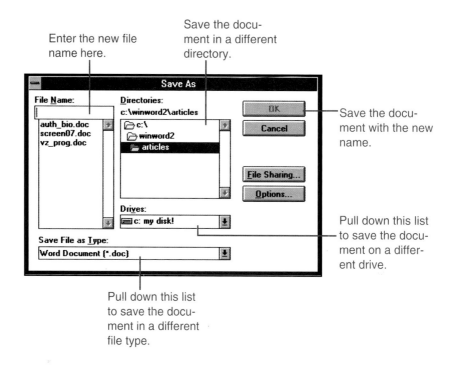

Enter the new file name here.

Save the document in a different directory.

Save the document with the new name.

Pull down this list to save the document on a different drive.

Pull down this list to save the document in a different file type.

Changing a Document's Name

1 Press **Alt+F** or click on File.

2 Press **A** or click on Save As.

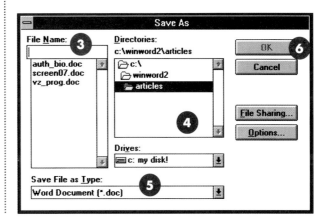

File
New...
Open...   Ctrl+F12
Close

Save   Shift+F12
Save As...   F12
Save All

Find File...
Summary Info...
Template...

Print Preview
Print...   Ctrl+Shift+F12
Print Merge...
Print Setup...

Exit   Alt+F4

1 SCREEN38.DOC
2 SCREEN24.DOC
3 SCREENS.DOC
4 SHOWWFW1.DOC

3 Enter the new file name.

4 To save the document in a different location, select a drive and/or directory.

5 Select a File Type if you want to save the document for use by another type of word processing program.

6 Press **Enter** or click **OK**.

Save As

File Name:
auth_bio.doc
screen07.doc
vz_prog.doc

Directories:
c:\winword2\articles
c:\
winword2
articles

OK
Cancel

File Sharing...
Options...

Drives:
c: my disk!

Save File as Type:
Word Document (*.doc)

LEARNING THE LINGO

File type: The format used to save the document on disk.

Creating, Editing, Saving, and Printing Documents

OPENING A DOCUMENT

Why Open a Document?

If you want to work on a document that you saved at an earlier time, you must open it. When you open a document it appears on your screen exactly as it was when you saved it. To open a document, issue the **File Open** command to display the Open dialog box.

Type the name of the file that you want to open here.

Select a directory in the Directories list to open a document in a different directory.

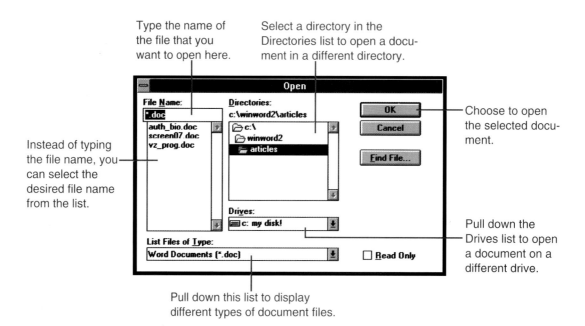

Instead of typing the file name, you can select the desired file name from the list.

Choose to open the selected document.

Pull down the Drives list to open a document on a different drive.

Pull down this list to display different types of document files.

Opening a Document

1️⃣ Press **Alt + F** or click **File**.

2️⃣ Press **O** or click **Open**.

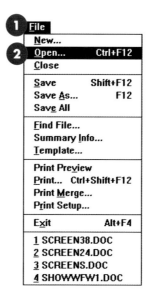

③ Switch to a different drive or directory if necessary.

④ Type the file name in the box, or click on it in the list.

⑤ Press **Enter** or click this button to open the file.

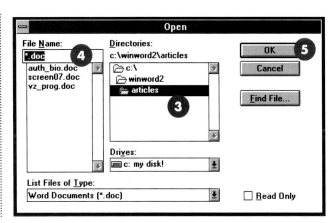

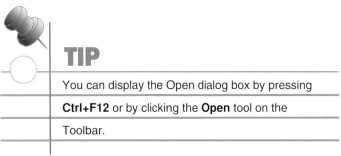

TIP

You can display the Open dialog box by pressing

Ctrl+F12 or by clicking the **Open** tool on the

Toolbar.

Creating, Editing, Saving, and Printing Documents

PRINTING AN ENTIRE DOCUMENT

Why Print Your Document?

Most documents must be printed to serve their intended purpose. A letter to a client, a memo for your employees, or a report for your supervisor isn't much use until it's printed on paper!

To print, use the **File** **P**rint command. Issuing this command displays the Print dialog box.

Choose the up or down arrow (or type a value) to print more than one copy.

Leave this list set to Document to print the document.

Choose this button or press Enter to start printing.

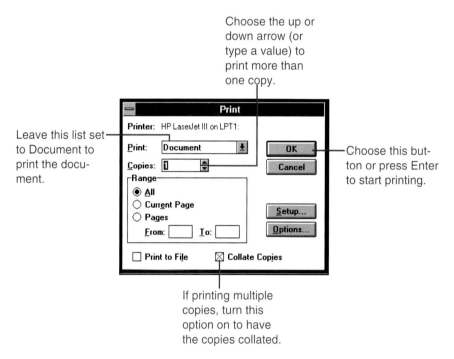

If printing multiple copies, turn this option on to have the copies collated.

TIP

For printing to work, your system must have a printer connected to it. The printer must be turned on, be loaded with paper, and set to "on-line."

Printing Your Document

1 Press **Alt+F** or click on **File**.

2 Press **P** or click on **Print**.

3 Enter a number or click the arrows to specify the desired number of copies.

4 Press **Enter** or click **OK**.

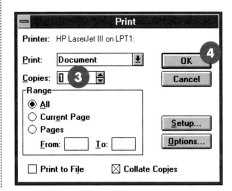

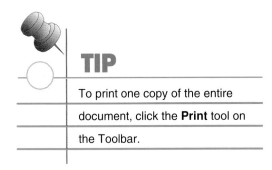

TIP

To print one copy of the entire document, click the **Print** tool on the Toolbar.

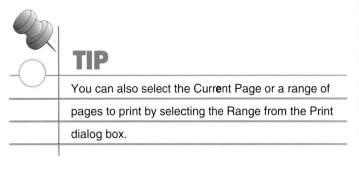

TIP

You can also select the Current Page or a range of pages to print by selecting the Range from the Print dialog box.

PRINTING AN ENTIRE DOCUMENT

Exercise

Enter the text shown in this figure and print it.

1 Issue the **File Print** command.

2 Press **Enter** or click **OK**.

3 As an alternative, click the **Print** tool on the Toolbar.

QUICK REFRESHER

Making dialog box selections

Color:
■ Auto

Drop-down list. Click on the down arrow to display the list. Click on the list item you want.

Copies: 1

Number box. Click the up or down arrow to increase or decrease the current value, or click in the box and type a value.

○ Up ● Down

Option button. Click on a button to turn it on. Turning on one option button turns off all others in the group.

Find What:

Text box. Click to position the I-beam in the box. Edit the existing entry or type a new one.

☐ Match Whole Word Only

Check box. Click on a box to turn it on or off.

CLOSING A DOCUMENT

Why Close a Document?

When you are finished working on a document you should close it. Closing a document does not exit Word; it just gets one particular document off your screen so you will have more room to work on other documents.

To Close a Document

1 Press **Alt+F** or click on **File**.

2 Press **C** or click on **Close**.

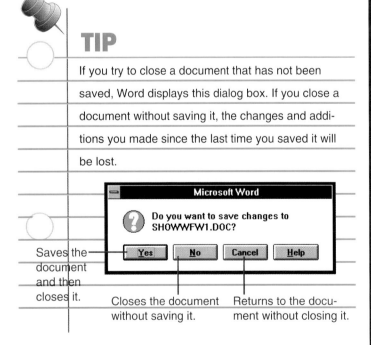

1 File
New...
Open...   Ctrl+F12
2 Close

Save   Shift+F12
Save As...   F12
Save All

Find File...
Summary Info...
Template...

Print Preview
Print... Ctrl+Shift+F12
Print Merge...
Print Setup...

Exit   Alt+F4

1 SHOWWFW1.DOC
2 SCREEN52.DOC
3 SCREEN38.DOC
4 SCREEN24.DOC

TIP

When you close all the open documents, you are left with a totally blank workspace. (If you suddenly only have two pull-down menus, it means there are no documents open.) At this point, you can either exit Word (**press F**ile E**x**it) or start a new document (**press F**ile **N**ew or click on this tool). See the task "Opening Multiple Documents" for more information.

TIP

If you try to close a document that has not been saved, Word displays this dialog box. If you close a document without saving it, the changes and additions you made since the last time you saved it will be lost.

```
Microsoft Word
(?)  Do you want to save changes to
     SHOWWFW1.DOC?

  [ Yes ]   [ No ]   [ Cancel ]   [ Help ]
```

Saves the document and then closes it.

Closes the document without saving it.

Returns to the document without closing it.

Creating, Editing, Saving, and Printing Documents

PART 3

Formatting
Your Document

In this section, you will learn how to control the formatting, or appearance, of your documents.
These tasks will help you to create attractive and effective documents.

- Using the Ribbon
- Formatting Characters
- Formatting Paragraphs
- Formatting Paragraphs Using the Ruler and Ribbon
- Creating Bulleted and Numbered Lists
- Setting Tab Stops
- Setting Page Margins
- Setting Paper Size and Orientation
- Assigning Styles
- Creating a Style
- Editing an Existing Style
- Inserting Page Numbers

USING THE RIBBON

What Is the Ribbon?

The Ribbon is displayed on your screen between the menu bar and the document. The Ribbon provides a quick method of applying certain kinds of formatting to your document. If the Ribbon is not visible, issue the **View Ribbon** command to display it.

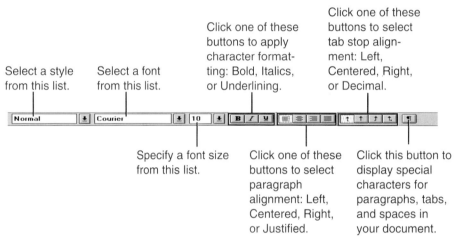

Select a style from this list.

Select a font from this list.

Click one of these buttons to apply character formatting: Bold, Italics, or Underlining.

Click one of these buttons to select tab stop alignment: Left, Centered, Right, or Decimal.

Specify a font size from this list.

Click one of these buttons to select paragraph alignment: Left, Centered, Right, or Justified.

Click this button to display special characters for paragraphs, tabs, and spaces in your document.

TIP

Refer to the tasks "Setting Tabs," "Formatting Characters," and "Formatting Paragraphs" for more information on using the Ribbon.

Using the Ribbon to Bold and Center Text

1 Select the paragraph.

2 Click on the **Bold** tool to make the characters bold.

3 Click on the **Center** tool to make the paragraph centered.

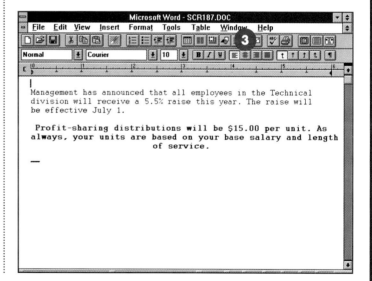

Formatting Your Document

FORMATTING CHARACTERS

Why Format Characters?

Formatting characters changes the font, size, and style (underline, italics, and so on) of the letters. You use character formatting to emphasize certain parts of your document and to improve its appearance. You can specify character formatting before you enter text; then as you type, the new text appears in the selected character style. You can also select a block of existing text and change its formatting.

To choose formatting options use the Format Character command. This displays the Character dialog box.

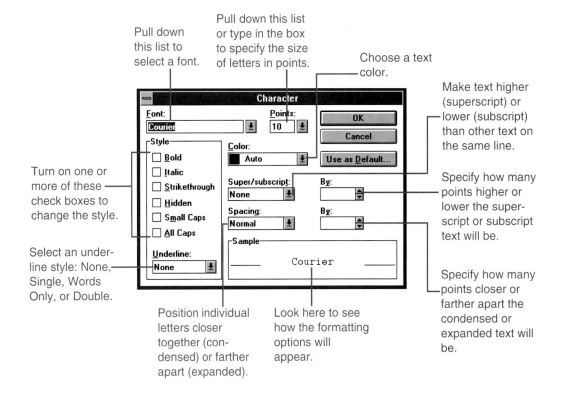

Pull down this list to select a font.

Pull down this list or type in the box to specify the size of letters in points.

Choose a text color.

Make text higher (superscript) or lower (subscript) than other text on the same line.

Turn on one or more of these check boxes to change the style.

Select an underline style: None, Single, Words Only, or Double.

Position individual letters closer together (condensed) or farther apart (expanded).

Look here to see how the formatting options will appear.

Specify how many points higher or lower the superscript or subscript text will be.

Specify how many points closer or farther apart the condensed or expanded text will be.

LEARNING THE LINGO

Font: A set of characters with a specific design.

Point: A measurement of character size and spacing. One point is 1/72 of an inch.

Strikethrough: A character style that makes the text look as if it were crossed out.

Formatting Characters

1 Position the insertion point where you want new text to appear, or select the text whose format you want to change.

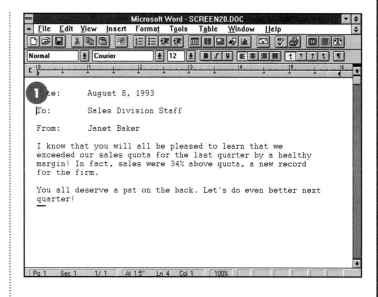

2 Press **Alt+T** or click on Forma**t**.

3 Press **C** or click on **C**haracter.

4 Select the desired character formatting options from the Character dialog box.

5 Press **Enter** or click **OK**.

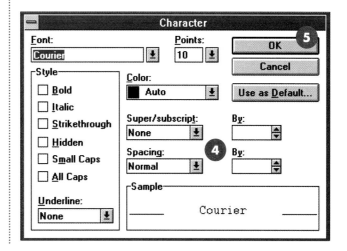

Formatting Your Document

FORMATTING CHARACTERS

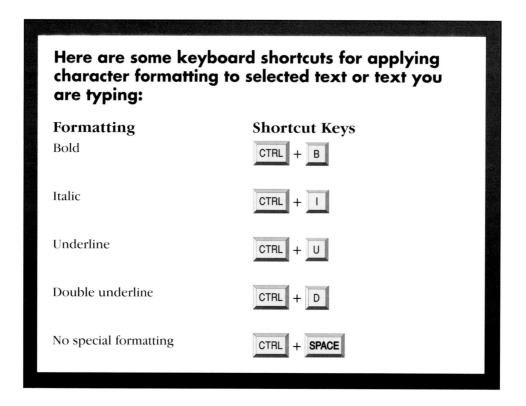

Here are some keyboard shortcuts for applying character formatting to selected text or text you are typing:

Formatting	Shortcut Keys
Bold	CTRL + B
Italic	CTRL + I
Underline	CTRL + U
Double underline	CTRL + D
No special formatting	CTRL + SPACE

TIP

You can quickly select character formatting using the Ribbon. If you can't see the Ribbon, press **Alt+V** and then press **B**, or click on **V**iew and then Ri**b**bon.

The Ribbon displays the font name and size for the text where the insertion point is located. If the text is Bold, Italic, or Underlined the corresponding button appears to be pressed.

Pull down this list to select a font.   Pull down this list, or type in a value, to select a point size..

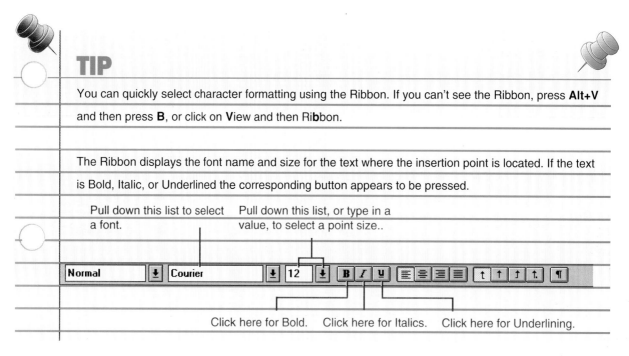

Click here for Bold.   Click here for Italics.   Click here for Underlining.

Exercise

Enter the text shown in this figure and practice changing the character formatting.

1 Select the first line and make it 18-point bold.

2 Select the second line and underline it.

3 Select the word **congratulations** and make it italic.

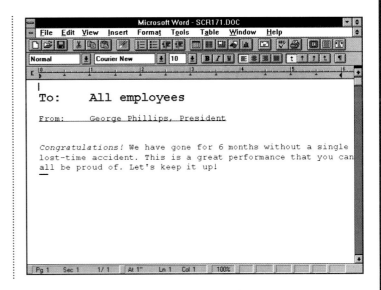

QUICK REFRESHER

Selecting text with the keyboard

Position the insertion point at the start of the text, press and hold **Shift**, and use the arrow keys to stretch the highlight.

Selecting text with the mouse

Position the I-beam at the start of the text, press and hold the left mouse button, drag the highlight to the end of the text, and release the mouse button.

Formatting Your Document

FORMATTING PARAGRAPHS

Why Format Paragraphs?

Paragraph formatting controls the appearance of entire paragraphs, such as the indentation, line spacing, and alignment. Paragraph formatting is an important part of your document's appearance. Remember that you mark the end of a paragraph, and the start of the next paragraph, by pressing Enter.

To set paragraph formatting, issue the Format Paragraph command, which displays the Paragraph dialog box.

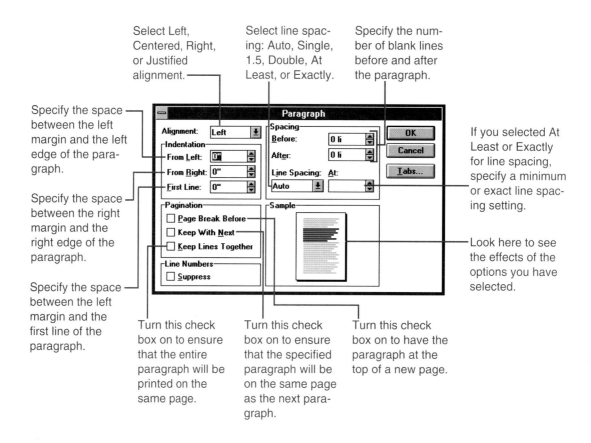

Select Left, Centered, Right, or Justified alignment.

Select line spacing: Auto, Single, 1.5, Double, At Least, or Exactly.

Specify the number of blank lines before and after the paragraph.

Specify the space between the left margin and the left edge of the paragraph.

Specify the space between the right margin and the right edge of the paragraph.

Specify the space between the left margin and the first line of the paragraph.

If you selected At Least or Exactly for line spacing, specify a minimum or exact line spacing setting.

Look here to see the effects of the options you have selected.

Turn this check box on to ensure that the entire paragraph will be printed on the same page.

Turn this check box on to ensure that the specified paragraph will be on the same page as the next paragraph.

Turn this check box on to have the paragraph at the top of a new page.

LEARNING THE LINGO

These terms are used for setting the Alignment option:

Left: The left edge of each line is even with the left margin.

Centered: Each line is centered on the page.

Right: The right edge of each line is even with the right margin.

Justified: Left and Right alignment combined.

Formatting Paragraphs

1 Select the paragraphs to format. For a single paragraph, place the insertion point anywhere in the paragraph or at the beginning of the paragraph before you start typing it.

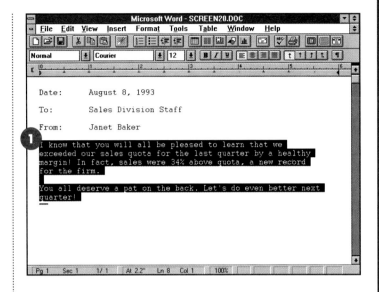

2 Press **Alt+T** or click on Format.

3 Press **P** or click on **P**aragraph.

4 Select the formatting options you want from the Paragraph dialog box.

5 Press **Enter** or click **OK**.

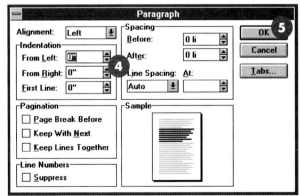

79

FORMATTING PARAGRAPHS

Exercise

Enter the text shown in the figure and change the paragraph formatting.

1 Set Alignment to Justified for all three paragraphs.

2 Change both the Left and Right indentation of the second paragraph to 1 inch.

3 Change the line spacing to Double for the entire document.

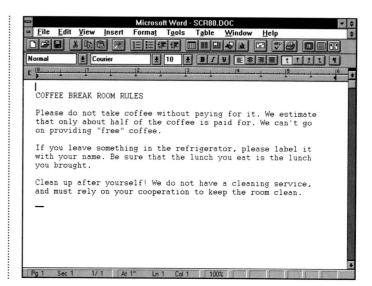

TIP

If you set Auto line spacing, Word makes each line as tall as the tallest character in the line. At Least line spacing sets a minimum line height that Word will increase if the line contains characters that are too tall to fit. Exact line spacing sets a line height that will not be changed. Characters that are too tall appear clipped off on-screen, and will overlap when printed.

TIP

To indent the first line of a paragraph, press **Tab** or click on the Indent tools on the Toolbar to indent or remove indents from the entire paragraph.

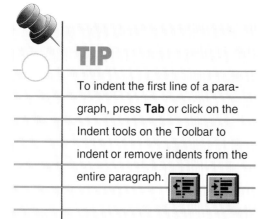

TIP

You can display the Paragraph dialog box by double-clicking on the top half of the Ruler.

To create a hanging indent, where the first line of the paragraph extends to the left more than all other lines, press **Ctrl+T**. To undo a hanging indent, press **Ctrl+G**.

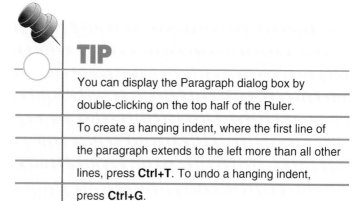

FORMATTING PARAGRAPHS USING THE RULER AND RIBBON

Why Use the Ruler and Ribbon for Formatting?

If you like working with the mouse, you can quickly format paragraphs using the Ruler and Ribbon. You cannot control all aspects of formatting with the Ruler and Ribbon, but you can set the most commonly used ones.

Click one of these buttons for Left, Centered, Right, or Justified alignment.

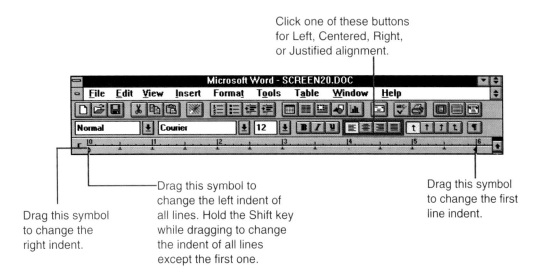

Drag this symbol to change the left indent of all lines. Hold the Shift key while dragging to change the indent of all lines except the first one.

Drag this symbol to change the first line indent.

Drag this symbol to change the right indent.

TIP

If necessary, press **Alt+V** and then press **B** to display the Ribbon, or press **Alt+V** and then press **R** to display the Ruler.

TIP

Indents are always measured relative to the page margins. See the task "Setting Page Margins" for more information.

Formatting Your Document

Setting Formatting with the Ruler and Ribbon

1 Select the paragraphs to format. For a single paragraph, place the insertion point anywhere in the paragraph.

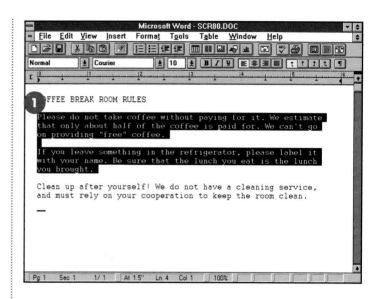

2 Click one of these buttons to set paragraph alignment.

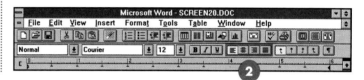

CREATING BULLETED AND NUMBERED LISTS

Why Use Bulleted and Numbered Lists?

Bulleted and numbered lists are common requirements for many types of documents. You can quickly turn a series of paragraphs into either a bulleted or numbered list.

A bulleted list is a list with a symbol to mark each paragraph. For example:

- This is point #1.
- This is point #2.
- This is point #3.

A numbered list is a list with sequentially-numbered paragraphs. For example:

1. This is step 1.
2. This is step 2.
3. This is step 3.

Bulleted and numbered lists use a hanging indent to make the symbol or number appear to be "hanging" from the paragraph. For example:

- This paragraph uses a hanging indent. The first line is set up to start a few spaces to the left of the subsequent lines, so the bullet appears to be hanging on the left side of the paragraph.

You can create hanging indents manually using the Format Paragraph command, but it is much easier to use Word's built-in bulleted and numbered list creation features.

LEARNING THE LINGO

Bullet: A symbol used to mark the beginning of a paragraph.

Hanging indent: A negative-indent (first line farther to the left than subsequent lines) that makes the first line appear to hang off the left edge of the paragraph.

CREATING BULLETED AND NUMBERED LISTS

Creating a Bulleted or Numbered List

1 Select the paragraph(s) that you want to convert into a list.

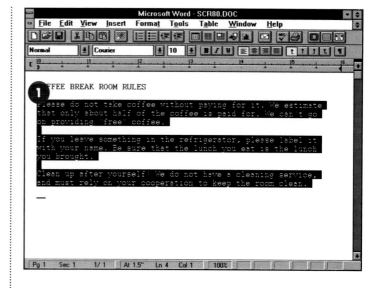

2 Select Tools and **then** Bullets and numbering. Or click on the **Number** or **Bullet** list tools on the Toolbar to create a numbered or bulleted list.

SETTING TAB STOPS

What Are Tab Stops?

Tab stops are specific locations on a line of text that are defined by Word or by you. Whenever you press the Tab key, the insertion point and any text to the right of it move over to the next tab stop. You use tab stops to control the indentation of text in your document.

Word provides default tab stops that are spaced one-half inch apart. You can add new tab stops, change the position of existing tab stops, or change tab stop alignment. To set or modify tab stops, issue the Format Tabs command to display the Tabs dialog box.

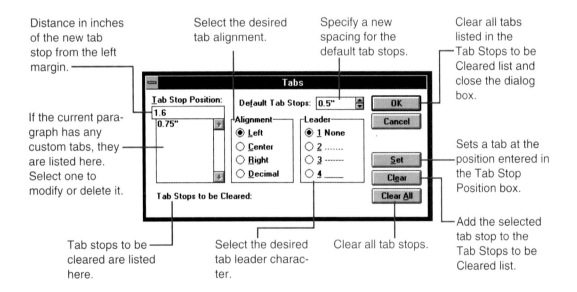

Distance in inches of the new tab stop from the left margin.

Select the desired tab alignment.

Specify a new spacing for the default tab stops.

Clear all tabs listed in the Tab Stops to be Cleared list and close the dialog box.

If the current paragraph has any custom tabs, they are listed here. Select one to modify or delete it.

Sets a tab at the position entered in the Tab Stop Position box.

Tab stops to be cleared are listed here.

Select the desired tab leader character.

Clear all tab stops.

Add the selected tab stop to the Tab Stops to be Cleared list.

LEARNING THE LINGO

Left tab: The left edge of text aligns at the tab stop.

Right tab: The right edge of text aligns at the tab stop.

Center tab: Text is centered at the tab stop.

Decimal tab: The decimal point aligns at the tab stop.

Leader character: A character, such as a hyphen, that fills the tab space between words.

Formatting Your Document

Setting Tab Stops

1 Move the insertion point to the location where you want the new tab stop to take effect, or select the paragraphs for the new tab stop.

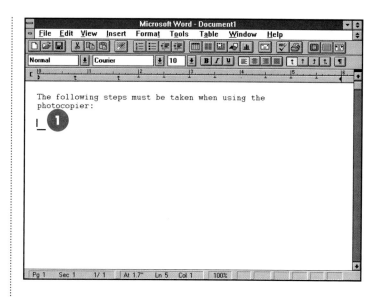

2 Press **Alt+T** or click on Forma**t**.

3 Press **T** or click on **T**abs.

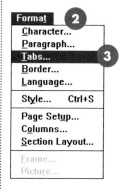

4 Enter the new tab stop position in inches.

5 Specify a new spacing for the default tab stops.

6 Select alignment and leader options.

7 Click **S**et to set the new tab stop.

8 Click **OK** to close the dialog box.

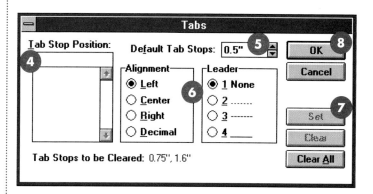

TIP

Tab stops apply to any paragraphs you have selected. Otherwise they apply from the insertion point onward.

You can set and clear custom tabs stops with the Ruler and mouse. If the Ruler is not visible, issue the **V**iew **R**uler command to display it. The Ruler displays each default tab and custom tab stop.

- To set a new tab stop, click the desired position on the lower half of the Ruler.
- To delete a custom tab stop, point at and drag it below the Ruler.
- To move a tab stop, point at and drag it to the new position on the Ruler.

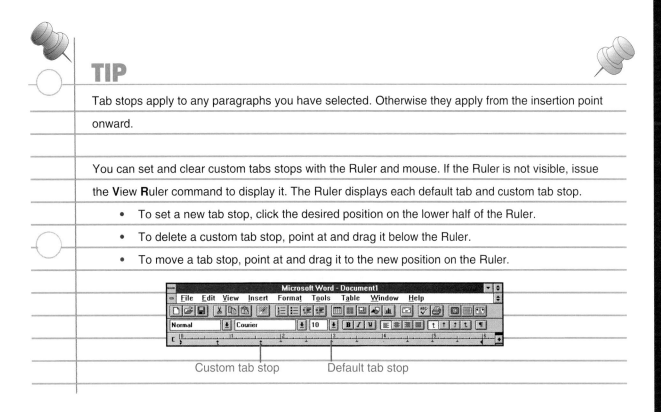

Custom tab stop   Default tab stop

Exercise

Enter the text shown in the figure, indenting the first line of each paragraph one tab stop. Move the insertion point to the start of the document and modify the tab stop settings as directed in the following steps.

1 Change the default tab stop spacing to 1 inch.

2 Insert a custom tab stop at 0.75 inch.

3 Delete the custom tab stop.

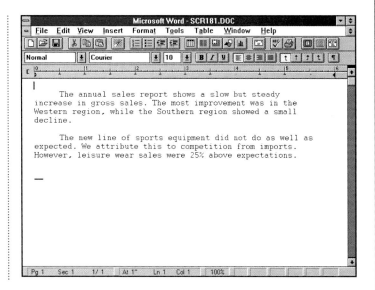

Formatting Your Document

SETTING PAGE MARGINS

What Are Page Margins?

Margins are the space between your text and the edges of the paper. Each page has four margins: Top, Bottom, Left, and Right.

Word's default margins are fine for most situations, but you can change them as needed for all or part of a document. For example, if you're writing a letter that almost fits on one page, you may be able to make it fit by decreasing all four margin settings by a fraction of an inch. Or if you're writing a very short letter, you can make it seem more substantial by increasing all four margins by a half-inch or so.

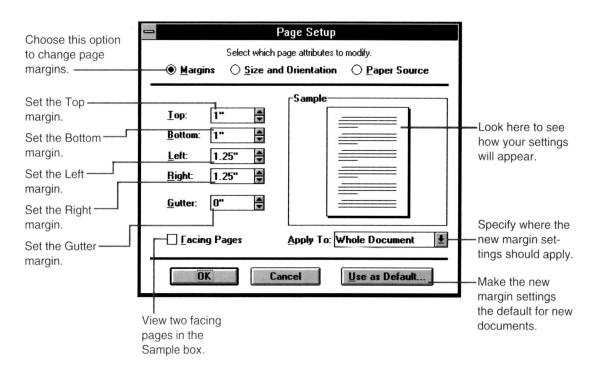

Choose this option to change page margins.

Set the Top margin.

Set the Bottom margin.

Set the Left margin.

Set the Right margin.

Set the Gutter margin.

View two facing pages in the Sample box.

Look here to see how your settings will appear.

Specify where the new margin settings should apply.

Make the new margin settings the default for new documents.

LEARNING THE LINGO

Gutter margin: Extra space added to the inside margins to allow for binding.

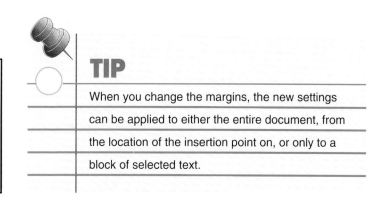

TIP

When you change the margins, the new settings can be applied to either the entire document, from the location of the insertion point on, or only to a block of selected text.

Changing Page Margins

1 If you want the new margins to apply to only part of the document, select the text or move the insertion point to where you want the new margins to start.

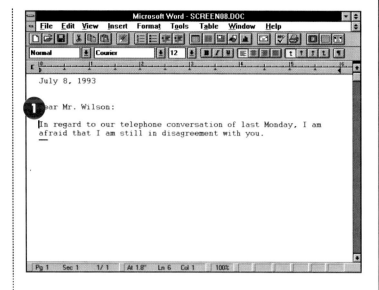

2 Press **Alt+T** or click Format.

3 Press **U** or click Page Setup.

4 If necessary click the **Margins** option button.

5 Enter the new values for the margins.

6 Specify the part of the document where you want the new settings to apply.

7 Press **Enter** or click **OK**.

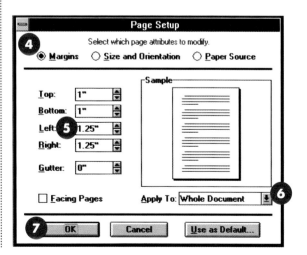

89

SETTING PAGE MARGINS

You can change the left and right margins of selected text using the Ruler. On the Ruler, click on the left margin marker to display the margin markers. Drag the left margin marker or the right margin marker to change the margins.

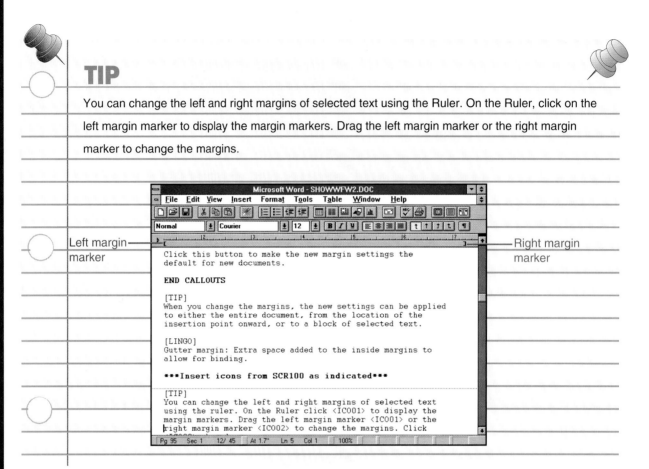

Left margin marker

Right margin marker

SETTING PAPER SIZE AND ORIENTATION

Why Change Paper Size and Orientation?

You must specify the size and orientation of your paper so that Word can print your document properly. Word's default is 8 1/2-by-11-inch paper in portrait orientation, which is fine for most documents. Your printer may offer other size and orientation options.

To specify paper size and orientation, issue the Format Page Setup command to display the Page Setup dialog box.

Select from pre-defined paper sizes.

Set paper size and orientation.

For a custom size, enter the width and height in these boxes or click the arrows to choose values.

Choose either Portrait or Landscape orientation.

Look here to see what your page will look like.

Specify whether the new settings will apply to the entire document or from the insertion point on.

Make the new settings the default for new documents.

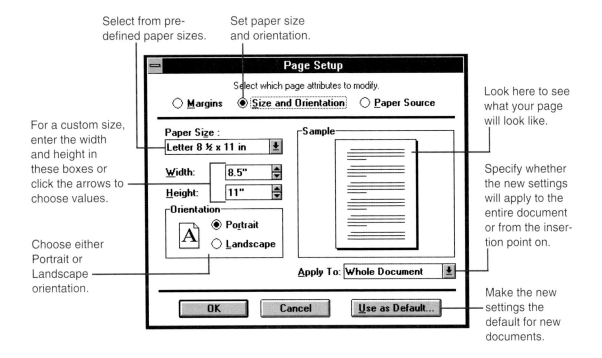

LEARNING THE LINGO

Portrait orientation: Lines of text are parallel to the paper's short edge.

Landscape orientation: Lines of text are parallel to the paper's long edge.

SETTING PAPER SIZE AND ORIENTATION

Changing Paper Size and Orientation

1 Press **Alt+T** or click Format.

2 Press **U** or click Page Setup.

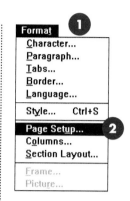

3 If necessary click the Size and Orientation option button.

4 Select the desired size and orientation options.

5 Specify the part of the document where you want the new settings to apply.

6 Press **Enter** or click **OK**.

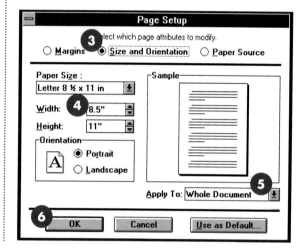

ASSIGNING STYLES

What Is a Style?

A style is a collection of formatting that has been assigned a name. A style can specify a certain font, line spacing, and indentation. For example, if you use a bold, centered, 24-point Courier heading in many reports, you could create a style called BOLDHEAD and then apply the style to each paragraph that you wanted to appear that way.

By assigning a style to a paragraph, you automatically apply all of the style's formatting to that paragraph. If you later go back and modify the style's formatting, the new formatting will automatically be applied to all paragraphs in the document with that style.

Word has a number of predefined styles, and you can also create your own. The default style is Normal.

How to Assign a Style to a Paragraph

1 Move the insertion point anywhere in the paragraph. Or to assign to multiple paragraphs, select the paragraphs.

2 Click the down arrow next to the Style box on the Ribbon.

3 Click the name of the style you want.

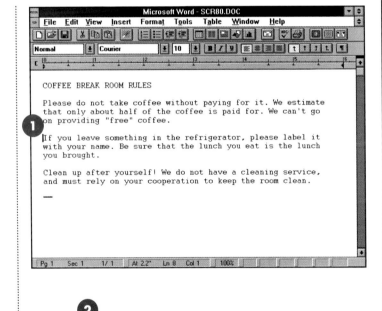

ASSIGNING STYLES

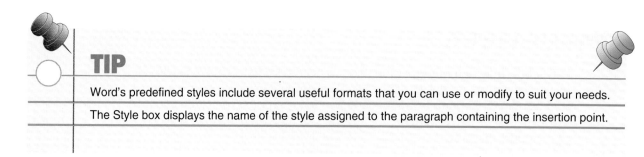

TIP

Word's predefined styles include several useful formats that you can use or modify to suit your needs.

The Style box displays the name of the style assigned to the paragraph containing the insertion point.

Exercise

Enter the text shown in the figure and practice assigning styles to the paragraphs.

1 Assign the style "Heading 1" to the first line.

2 Assign the style "Heading 2" to the last line.

3 Assign the style "Normal" to the paragraphs between the first and last lines.

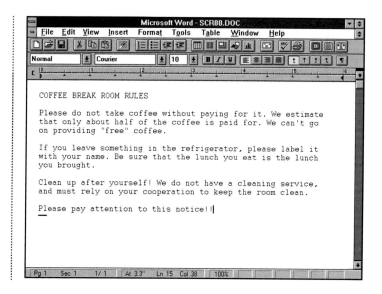

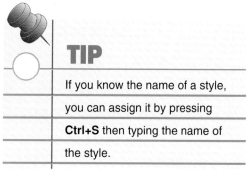

TIP

If you know the name of a style, you can assign it by pressing **Ctrl+S** then typing the name of the style.

QUICK REFRESHER

Selecting Paragraphs

To select one paragraph, double-click in the selection bar to the left of the paragraph.

To select multiple paragraphs, click next to the first line of the first paragraph in the selection bar, and then drag to the last line of the last paragraph.

CREATING A STYLE

Why Create Styles?

When you create a style, you assign a single name to a group of attributes—for example, FOOTNOTE style might be 10-point Arial italic with a hanging indent. Then when you need a paragraph to be formatted in that style, you simply apply the style, rather than setting up each format attribute separately.

You are not limited to the styles that come with Word; you can create your own. To create a style, apply the desired formatting to a paragraph. With the insertion point in the paragraph, issue the Format Style command to display the Style dialog box.

Select these check boxes to make the shortcut key work in combination with Ctrl and/or Shift.

Enter the new style name here.

Click this button to finish defining the style.

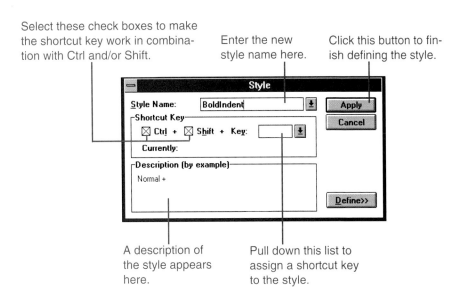

A description of the style appears here.

Pull down this list to assign a shortcut key to the style.

LEARNING THE LINGO

Shortcut Key: A key combination that you can press to quickly execute a command, apply a style, or perform some other action.

Formatting Your Document

CREATING A STYLE

How to Create a Style

1 Format a paragraph with the formatting that you want in the new style. Be sure the insertion point is in the paragraph.

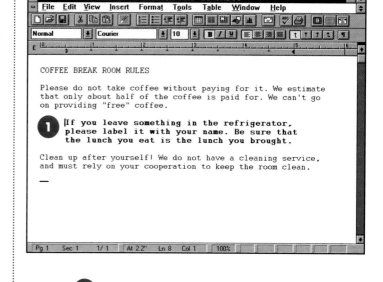

2 Press **Alt+T** or click Format.

3 Press **Y** or click Style.

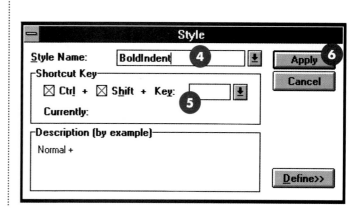

4 Enter the new style name in the **Style Name** box.

5 If you want to assign a shortcut key combination to the style, enter it under Shortcut Key.

6 Click on the **Apply** button to save the new style.

Exercise

Enter the paragraph shown in the figure. Format the paragraph and create a new style based on the formatting.

1 Indent the paragraph 0.5 inches from the left.

2 Select the entire paragraph and press **Ctrl+U** to underline it.

3 Press **Ctrl+S** to activate the Style box.

4 Type **Bold Indent** and press **Enter**.

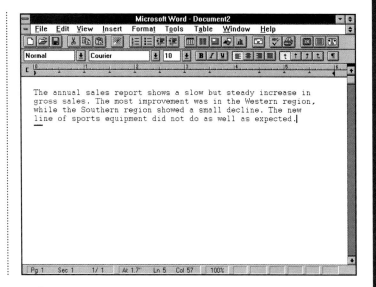

TIP

To quickly create a style based on the current paragraph's formatting, press **Ctrl+S**, type the new style name, and press **Enter**. If you press Ctrl+S when the Ribbon is not visible, Word displays Which Style? on the status bar. Enter the style name and press **Enter**. With the mouse, double-click the style box on the Ribbon, type the new style name, and then click anywhere outside the style box.

Formatting Your Document

EDITING AN EXISTING STYLE

Why Edit a Style?

When you edit a style you change the formatting commands that are associated with the style name. By editing a style you can quickly change the formatting of all the paragraphs in the document that have been assigned that style.

To change a style, you first issue the Format Style command to display the Style dialog box. Click the **Define** button to display the dialog box shown in the figure.

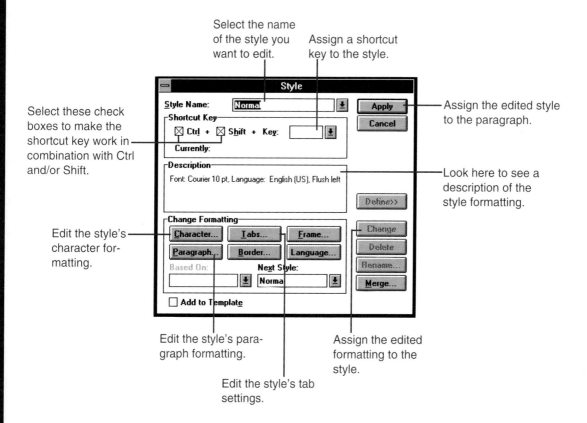

Select the name of the style you want to edit.

Assign a shortcut key to the style.

Select these check boxes to make the shortcut key work in combination with Ctrl and/or Shift.

Edit the style's character formatting.

Assign the edited style to the paragraph.

Look here to see a description of the style formatting.

Assign the edited formatting to the style.

Edit the style's paragraph formatting.

Edit the style's tab settings.

To Edit a Style

1 Press **Alt+T** or click on Forma**t**.

2 Press **Y** or click on Style.

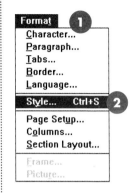

3 Choose the **D**efine button by pressing **Alt+D** or clicking on the Define button.

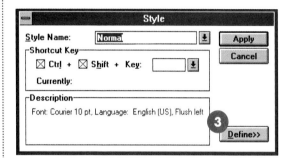

4 Select the style to edit.

5 Change the style's character or paragraph formatting.

6 Change the style's tab settings.

7 Assign a shortcut key to the style.

8 View a description of the style formatting.

9 Click on the Change button to assign the edited formatting to the style.

10 Click on the Apply button to assign the edited style to the current paragraph.

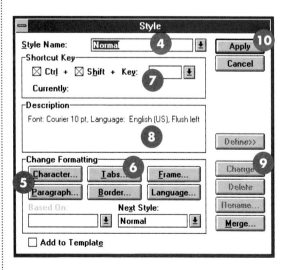

Formatting Your Document

INSERTING PAGE NUMBERS

Using Page Numbers

Word can automatically number the pages in a document, keeping track of changes and placing the numbers in a position on the page that you specify. You can also select from several different page number formats.

To add page numbers to a document, issue the **Insert Page Numbers** command to display the Page Numbers dialog box.

Select an option to place the page numbers at the top or bottom of each page.

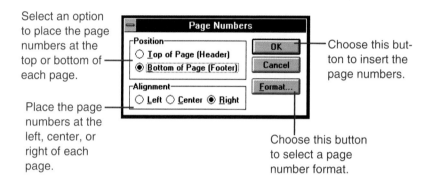

Choose this button to insert the page numbers.

Place the page numbers at the left, center, or right of each page.

Choose this button to select a page number format.

Select a page number format.

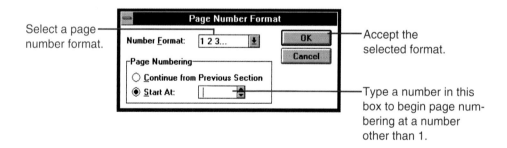

Accept the selected format.

Type a number in this box to begin page numbering at a number other than 1.

Inserting Page Numbers

1 Press **Alt+I** or click on Insert.

2 Press **U** or click on Page Numbers.

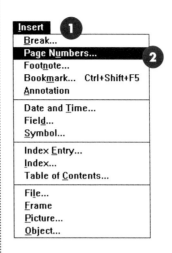

3 Select a position and alignment for the page numbers.

4 Press **T** or click Format to select a page number format.

5 Press **Enter** or click **OK**.

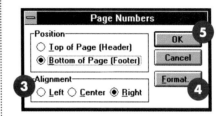

Formatting Your Document

PART 4

Beyond the Basics

In this section, you will learn some of the Word's more advanced features. These features can help you work more accurately and efficiently toward the creation of impressive professional documents.

- Changing the Document Display Mode

- Using Draft Mode

- Creating Your Own Template

- Modifying a Template

- Storing Text in a Glossary

- Inserting a Glossary Entry into a Document

- Editing a Glossary Entry

- Checking Your Spelling

- Using Your Thesaurus

- Print Preview

CHANGING THE DOCUMENT DISPLAY MODE

What Is the Document Display Mode?

The document display mode determines how your document is displayed on the screen. Each mode is suitable for certain types of editing and writing tasks. There are three basic display modes available.

In Normal mode, all text formatting (fonts, underline, and so on) is displayed, but the page layout is simplified to make typing and editing easier. Normal mode is suitable for most of your daily work.

Sales Promotion Plan

Print Advertising
Full-page color ads in six major magazines, plus half-page
ads in metropolitan newspapers.

Broadcast Advertising
Thirty second commercials during the evening news broadcast
on all 3 networks.

Direct Mail
Over two million pamphlets mailed to targeted, upper income
households.

In Outline mode, text is displayed organized by style headings. Outline mode is suitable for creating outlines and for viewing the organization of a document.

⬦ Sales Promotion Plan

   ⬦ **Print Advertising**
      ▫ Full-page color ads in six major magazines, plus
        half-page ads in metropolitan newspapers.

   ⬦ **Broadcast Advertising**
      ▫ Thirty second commercials during the evening news
        broadcast on all 3 networks.

   ⬦ **Direct Mail**
      ▫ Over two million pamphlets mailed to targeted,
        upper income households.

When you use Page Layout mode, text is displayed exactly as it will be printed. Page Layout mode is suitable for fine-tuning the appearance of your document.

When you use Page Layout mode, text is displayed exactly as it will be printed. Page Layout mode is suitable for fine-tuning the appearance of your document.

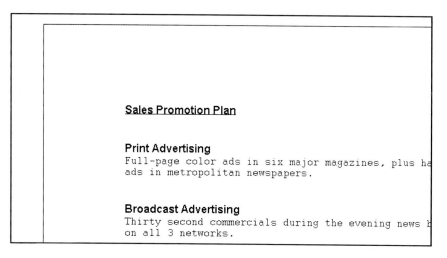

Changing the Document Display mode

1 Press **Alt+V** or click **View**.

2 Press **N** or click **Normal** for Normal view mode. Press **O** or click **Outline** for Outline view mode. Press P or click Page Layout for Page Layout view mode.

TIP

On the View menu, a bullet is displayed next to the view mode currently in effect.

TIP

To use Outline mode you must assign Word's pre-defined heading styles (Heading 1, Heading 2, and so on) to your document's headings. Paragraphs assigned the Heading 1 style become the top level heads in Outline Mode, and so on. For more information on assigning the heading styles, see the task "Assigning Styles."

Beyond the Basics

USING DRAFT MODE

Why Use Draft Mode?

In Draft mode, Word displays text on-screen without formatting, using a single standardized font. Character formatting, such as bold and italics, is indicated by underlining. Use Draft mode to allow the fastest possible scrolling and editing, and to make it easier to read and select text that is in a small font size. Draft mode is useful when you are concentrating on the content of a document rather than on its appearance. Later, when you want to see the finished product, you can change to Normal or Page Layout mode.

In Draft mode, character formatting is indicated by an underline.

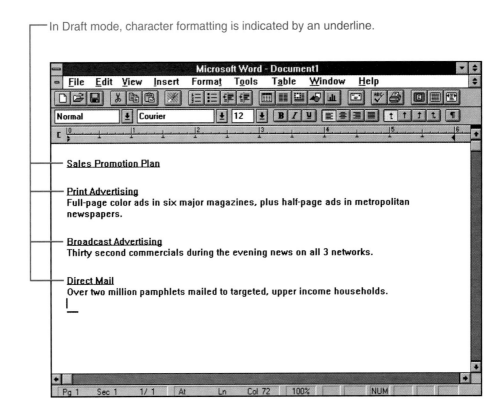

Using Draft Mode

1 Press **Alt+V** or click on View.

2 Press **D** or click on **D**raft to toggle Draft mode on or off.

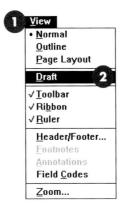

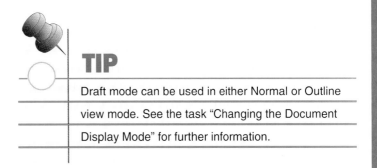

TIP

Draft mode can be used in either Normal or Outline view mode. See the task "Changing the Document Display Mode" for further information.

Beyond the Basics

CREATING YOUR OWN TEMPLATE

When Should You Create Your Own Templates?

If you create multiple documents that have a similar format, creating and using a template for those documents can save you a lot of time. Good candidates for a template would be a FAX cover sheet, a memo form, or a purchase requisition. With a template for documents such as these, you only need to type the parts that are different each time you create a new document.

Creating a template is no different than creating a document. You insert the text and graphics, and define the styles, macros, and glossaries, that you want in all documents based on the new template. Word saves templates with a name you assign and the .DOT extension.

To create a template, issue the **File New** command to display the New dialog box.

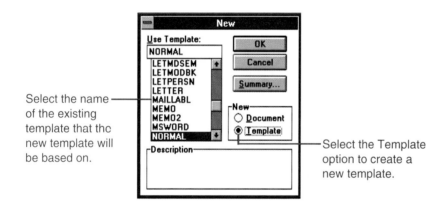

Select the name of the existing template that the new template will be based on.

Select the Template option to create a new template.

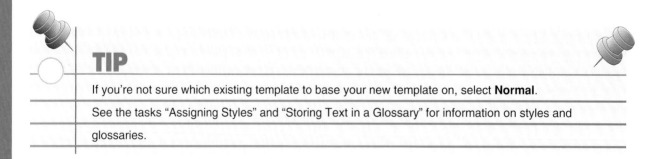

TIP

If you're not sure which existing template to base your new template on, select **Normal**.

See the tasks "Assigning Styles" and "Storing Text in a Glossary" for information on styles and glossaries.

How to Create a New Template

1 Press **Alt+F** or click on **File**.

2 Press **N** or click on **New**.

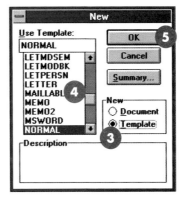

3 Select the Template option by pressing **Alt+T** or clicking on Template.

4 Select the existing template on which you want to base the new template.

5 Press **Enter** or click **OK**.

6 Enter the text, formatting, and styles that you want in the template.

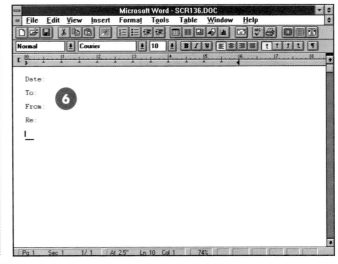

Beyond the Basics

CREATING YOUR OWN TEMPLATE

7 Press **Alt+F** or click on File.

8 Press **S** or click on Save.

9 Enter a 1-8 character name for the template.

10 Press **Enter** or click **OK**.

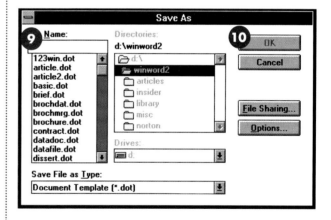

11 Enter a title for the template, if desired.

12 Press **Enter** or click **OK**.

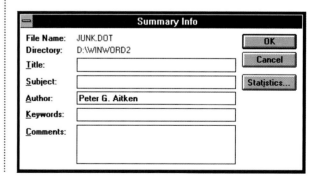

MODIFYING A TEMPLATE

When Should You Modify a Template?

You can modify a template when you want to make a change to the text, styles, or glossaries that will be part of all documents that are based on the template. A template can be opened, modified, and saved just like any other Word document. Any changes you make will appear in all documents subsequently created using the template. Documents previously created with the template will not be affected, but you can reapply a template to an old document after you've changed the template.

To modify a template you must open it using the File Open command. Issuing this command displays the Open dialog box.

Type the name of the template, or select it from the list.

Select Document Templates in the List Files of Type list.

Choose OK to open the selected template.

Open a template in a different directory.

Pull down this list to open a template on a different drive.

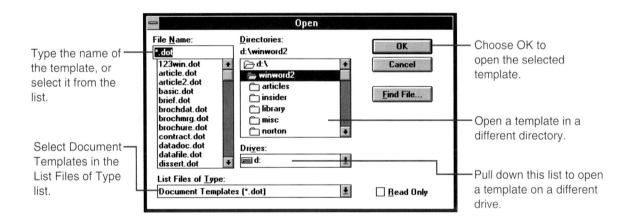

How to Modify a Template

1 Press **Alt+F** or click on File.

2 Press **O** or click on **Open**.

Beyond the Basics

MODIFYING A TEMPLATE

3 Press **Alt+T** or click on the down arrow to pull down the List Files of **T**ype list and click on **Document Templates (*.DOT)**.

4 Select a different drive and/or directory if necessary.

5 Enter the template name here, or click the name in the list.

6 Press **Enter** or click **OK**.

7 Use the normal editing procedures to make the desired changes in the template.

8 Press **Alt+F** or click on **F**ile.

9 Press **S** or click on **S**ave.

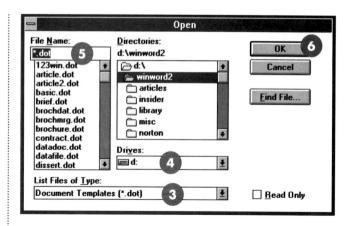

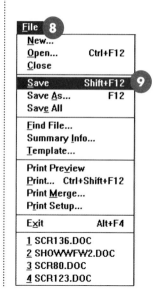

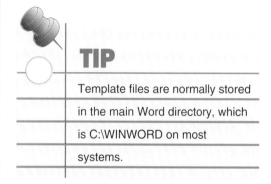

TIP

Template files are normally stored in the main Word directory, which is C:\WINWORD on most systems.

112

STORING TEXT IN A GLOSSARY

What Is a Glossary?

A glossary entry is a section of text that you assign a name to and store for later insertion into documents. A glossary entry can be of any length, and can contain any formatting that you like. Once stored, a glossary entry can be inserted into a document with only a few keystrokes, saving you the time of typing and formatting the text again.

To create a glossary entry, select the text you want in the entry and then issue the **E**dit **G**lossary command to display the Glossary dialog box.

Type the name for the glossary entry here.

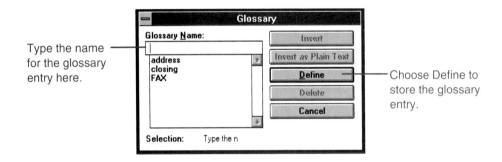

Choose Define to store the glossary entry.

TIP

If you want a glossary entry to include paragraph formatting, be sure to select the entire paragraph when you create the glossary entry.

TIP

Glossary entries are very useful for frequently used sections of text, such as a letter's salutation, your return address, your name or your company's name, or a contract clause.

STORING TEXT IN A GLOSSARY

How to Create a Glossary Entry

1 Type the text you want in the glossary entry and apply any desired formatting.

2 Select the text.

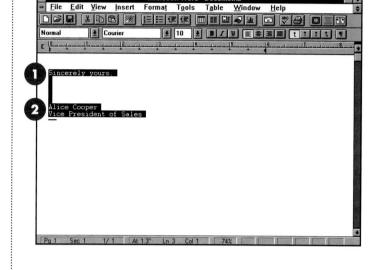

3 Press **Alt+E** or click on **Edit**.

4 Press **O** or click on **Glossary**.

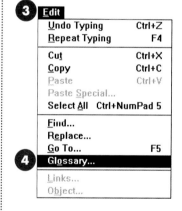

5 Type the name for the glossary entry.

6 Press **Alt+D** or click on the **Define** button to store the entry.

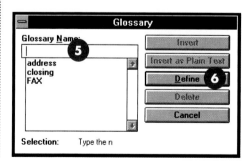

114

Exercise

Enter your own name and address, as shown in the figure, and store it as a glossary entry.

1 Select the text.

2 Issue the **E**dit Gl**o**ssary command to display the Glossary dialog box.

3 Enter the glossary name "address" in the Glossary **N**ame box.

4 Click **Define** or press **Enter**.

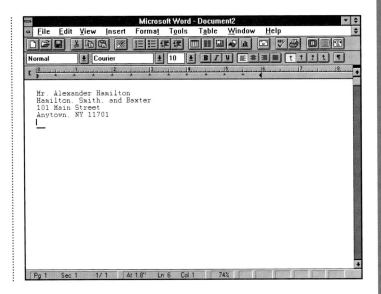

Beyond the Basics

INSERTING A GLOSSARY ENTRY INTO A DOCUMENT

Inserting Glossary Entries

You can insert any glossary entry in any location in your document. You can insert the glossary entry complete with its original formatting, or you can insert it as plain text so it will adopt the formatting of the text around it.

Choose **E**dit Gl**o**ssary to display the glossary dialog box.

Type the name of the glossary entry here.

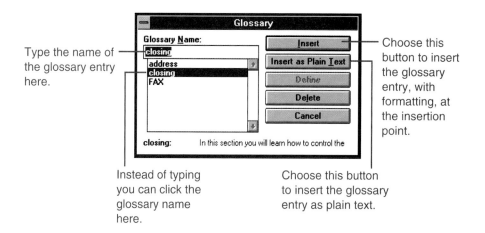

Choose this button to insert the glossary entry, with formatting, at the insertion point.

Instead of typing you can click the glossary name here.

Choose this button to insert the glossary entry as plain text.

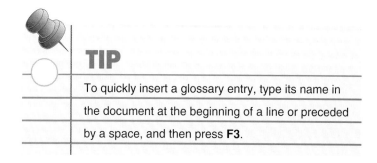

TIP

To quickly insert a glossary entry, type its name in the document at the beginning of a line or preceded by a space, and then press **F3**.

116

INSERTING A GLOSSARY ENTRY INTO A DOCUMENT

Inserting a Glossary Entry

1 Position the insertion point where you want the glossary entry to be inserted.

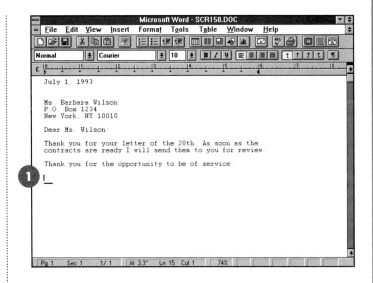

2 Press **Alt+E** or click on **E**dit.

3 Press **O** or click on Gl**o**ssary.

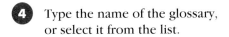
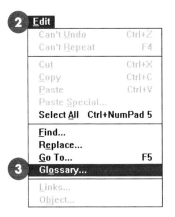

4 Type the name of the glossary, or select it from the list.

5 Press **Alt+I** or click on the **I**nsert button to insert the glossary with its formatting.

6 Press **Alt+T** or click on the Insert as Plain **T**ext button to insert the glossary as plain text.

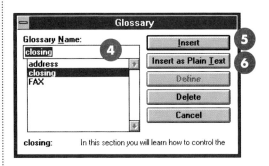

Beyond the Basics

EDITING A GLOSSARY ENTRY

Why Edit a Glossary Entry?

You can edit a glossary entry when you want to modify the text and/or formatting of the entry. After you edit an entry, subsequent insertions will reflect the changes that you made. Editing a glossary entry does not affect documents where the entry was previously inserted.

To edit a glossary entry, insert it in a document, make the desired changes and issue the Edit Glossary command to display the Glossary dialog box.

Type the name of the edited glossary here.

Instead of typing you can select the name from this list.

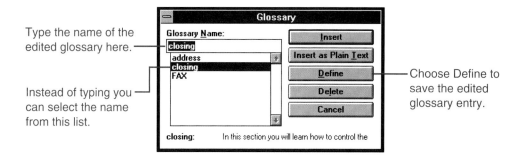

Choose Define to save the edited glossary entry.

Editing a Glossary Entry

1 Press **Alt+E** or click on **Edit**.

2 Press **O** or click on **Glossary**.

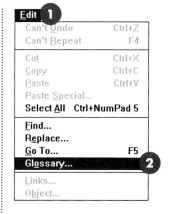

3 Type the name of the glossary to edit, or select it from the list.

4 Choose **Insert**.

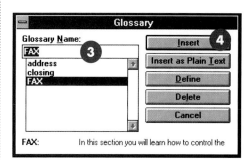

118

5 Edit the glossary text and formatting as desired, and then select the glossary text.

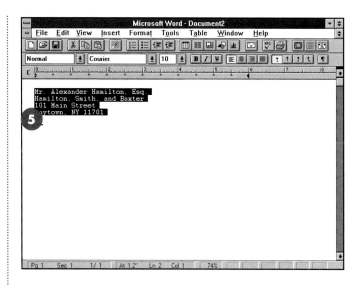

6 Press **Alt+E** or click on **E**dit.

7 Press **O** or click on Gl**o**ssary.

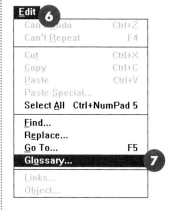

8 Type the original glossary name, or select it from the list.

9 Choose **D**efine.

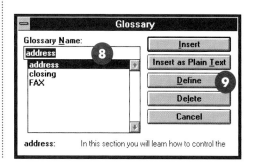

Beyond the Basics

10 Press **Y** or click on **Yes**.

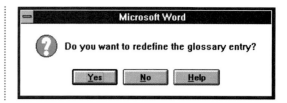

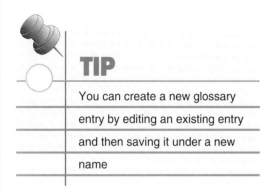

TIP

You can create a new glossary

entry by editing an existing entry

and then saving it under a new

name

CHECKING YOUR SPELLING

Why Check Your Spelling?

Even the best spellers make spelling errors, even if it's only a typographical error. Word's spelling checker can scan all or part of your document, reporting each word not found in its dictionary. You can ignore the word, add it to the dictionary, or use one of Word's suggested replacements.

To check a document's spelling select the Tools Spelling command. When Word finds a word not in its dictionary, it highlights the word in the document and displays the Spelling dialog box.

The misspelled word is displayed here.

Ignore the word.

A suggested replacement is listed here.

Ignore all occurrences of the word.

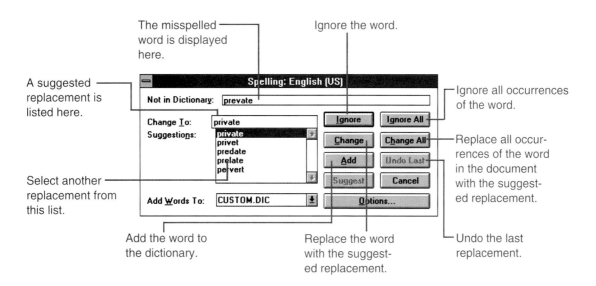

Select another replacement from this list.

Replace all occurrences of the word in the document with the suggested replacement.

Add the word to the dictionary.

Replace the word with the suggested replacement.

Undo the last replacement.

Checking Spelling

1 Press **Ctrl+Home** to move the insertion point to the start of the document.

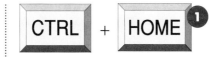

Beyond the Basics

CHECKING YOUR SPELLING

2 Press **Alt+O** or click on Tools.

3 Press **S** or click on **Spelling**.

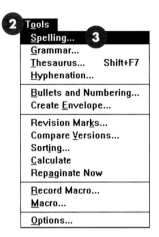

4 Each word not found in the dictionary is displayed.

5 Enter a replacement word, or select it from the list.

6 Press **Alt+I** or **Alt+G**, or click **I**gnore or **I**gnore All to ignore one or all occurrences of the word.

7 Press **Alt+A** or click on **A**dd to add the word to the dictionary.

8 Press **Alt+C** or **Alt+H**, or click **C**hange or C**h**ange all to replace one or all occurrences of the word with the suggested replacement.

9 Press **Alt+U** or click **U**ndo **Last** to undo the last replacement.

10 Click **Cancel** to end the spelling check operation.

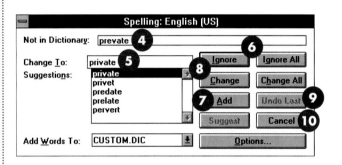

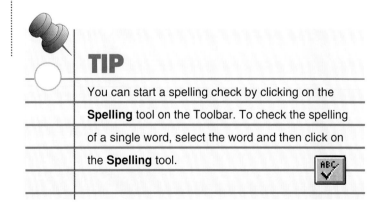

TIP

You can start a spelling check by clicking on the **Spelling** tool on the Toolbar. To check the spelling of a single word, select the word and then click on the **Spelling** tool.

USING THE THESAURUS

What Is a Thesaurus?

A thesaurus is used to look up synonyms for words, that is, words that have the same or a similar meaning. You can use Word's thesaurus to add variety to your writing, and to help you find the best word to use in a particular situation.

To use the thesaurus, position the insertion point in or just to the left of the word you want to look up, and then issue the Tools Thesaurus command. This command displays the Thesaurus dialog box.

The word you are looking up is displayed here.

The word selected in the Synonym list is displayed here.

Look up synonyms for the word in the Replace With box.

Different meanings for the word are displayed here. Select the one you are interested in.

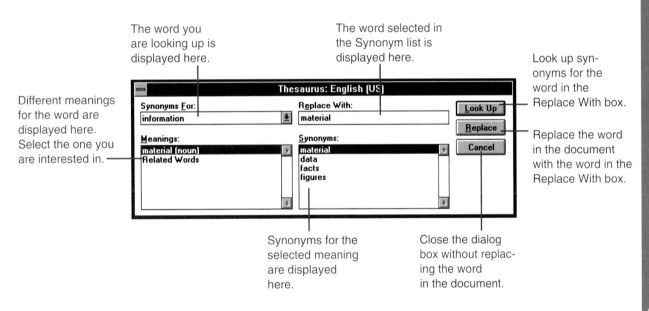

Synonyms for the selected meaning are displayed here.

Replace the word in the document with the word in the Replace With box.

Close the dialog box without replacing the word in the document.

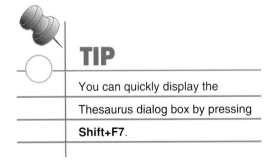

TIP

You can quickly display the

Thesaurus dialog box by pressing

Shift+F7.

Using the Thesaurus

1 Position the insertion point in or next to the word of interest in the document.

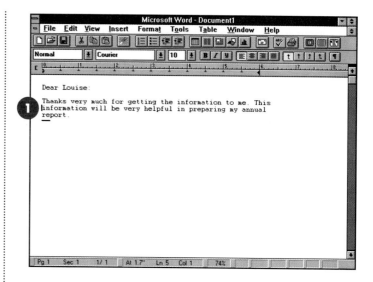

2 Press **Alt+O** or click on **T**ools.

3 Press **T** or click on **T**hesaurus.

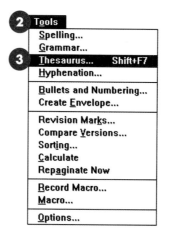

4 Select the proper meaning of the word.

5 Select the desired synonym.

6 Press **Enter** or click **R**eplace.

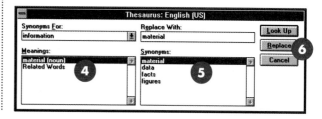

PRINT PREVIEW

Why Use Print Preview?

Print Preview shows you on-screen exactly how your document will look when it is printed. You can view one or two entire pages on-screen at the same time, which lets you evaluate the appearance of margins and page breaks. You cannot edit a document's text or formatting in Print Preview, but you can change margin settings.

To use Print Preview, issue the File Print Preview command. The page containing the insertion point will be displayed.

Print the document.　　View two adjacent pages.　　Close Print Preview and return to the document.

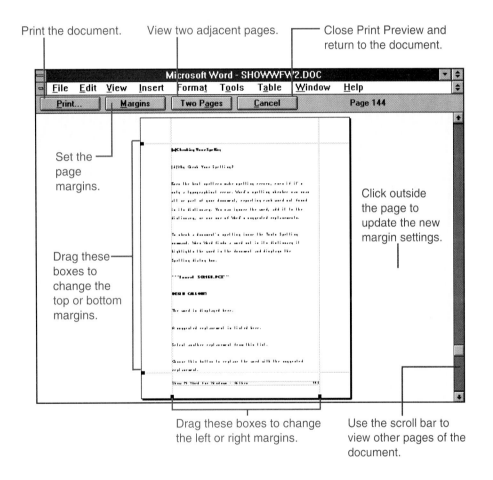

Set the page margins.

Drag these boxes to change the top or bottom margins.

Click outside the page to update the new margin settings.

Drag these boxes to change the left or right margins.

Use the scroll bar to view other pages of the document.

TIP

If you want to be able to edit the document while viewing it as it will be printed, use the Page Layout display mode. See the task "Changing the Document Display Mode" for details.

125

Beyond the Basics

PRINT PREVIEW

Using Print Preview

1 Press **Alt+F** or click on **F**ile.

2 Press **V** or click on Print Preview.

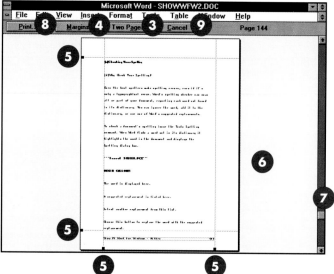

3 Press **A** or click on Two Pages to view two pages.

4 Press **M** or click on **M**argins to set the margins.

5 Point at a handle and drag it to change a margin setting.

6 Click outside the page to update the margins.

7 Click the scroll bar or press **PgUp** or **PgDn** to view other pages.

8 Press **P** or click on **P**rint to print the document.

9 Press **C** or click on **C**ancel to close Print Preview.

WORD FOR WINDOWS INSTALLATION

Before you can use Microsoft Word to create and edit documents, the program must be installed on your computer. The installation may have already been performed, in which case you are all set and can skip this section. If not, you will need to install the program. This is not difficult to do, and shouldn't take longer than 30 minutes.

You will need the diskettes that came with the Microsoft Word package. These are either 3 1/2- or 5 1/4-inch diskettes that are labeled Disk 1, Disk 2, and so on. Once you have located the diskettes, you are ready to begin.

1 If necessary, turn on your computer and start Windows.

2 Place installation Disk 1 in your computer's diskette drive.

3 From the Program Manager screen press **Alt+F** or click **File** to display the File menu.

4 Select **R**un from the File menu by pressing **R** or clicking **R**un. This will display the Run dialog box.

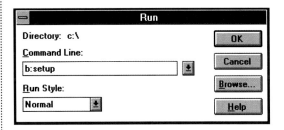

5 In the Command **L**ine text box type **a:setup** (if you placed the diskette in drive A:) or **b:setup** (if you placed the diskette in drive B:), and then press **Enter** or click **OK**.

6 The Setup program displays the Microsoft Word Setup dialog box, asking which directory Word should be installed in. The default directory is C:\WINWORD. Unless you have a specific reason to install Word in another directory, you should accept this by pressing **Enter** or clicking Continue.

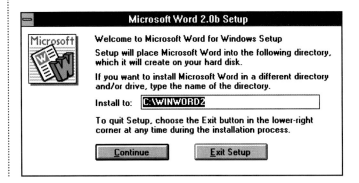

127

7 Next the Setup program gives you a choice of three installation options. Select **Complete Installation** by clicking the corresponding button.

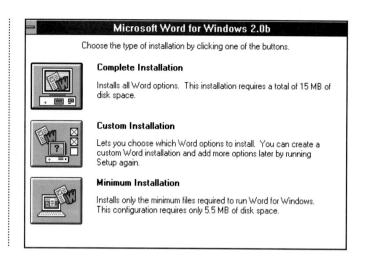

The Setup program will now begin copying the necessary files from the installation diskettes to your computer's hard disk. All you need to do is follow the instructions on-screen, changing diskettes when prompted.

When the installation is complete, you will return to the Program Manager screen. You are now ready to run Word!

Glossary

Center tab: Text is centered at the tab stop.

Centered paragraph alignment: Each line is centered on the page.

Clipboard: A temporary storage area built into most Windows-based programs. You can put a selection into the Clipboard with the Cut or Copy commands, and retrieve a selection from the Clipboard with the Paste command.

Copy: To duplicate a section of text and insert it in a new location. You end up with two copies of the text, one in the original location and one in the new location.

Decimal tab: The decimal point aligns at the tab stop.

Direction: In a Find operation, Up searches backward from the insertion point, and Down searches forward from the insertion point.

Document: The text that you are writing or editing—a letter, memo, report, and so on. No matter how many or how few characters, each group of text saved together in a file is a document.

Ellipsis: Three dots, or periods, following a menu command, which indicate that a dialog box will follow.

End of document marker: A short horizontal line that marks the end of the document.

File name: A name assigned to a document stored on disk. You designate the first part of the name, up to 8 characters. Word automatically adds the extension ".DOC" at the end of the file name.

File type: The format used to save the document on disk.

Font: A set of characters with a specific design.

Glossary: A "holding area" for bits of text that you want to use over and over again. When you copy text to a glossary, the text is available to be pasted into any document at any location.

Gutter margin: Extra space added to the inside margins on each page to allow for binding.

Highlighted text: Text that has been selected for some action. It appears with the colors "reversed" to show that it is specially marked.

Icon: A small picture on-screen that represents a program, an action you can take, or a piece of information.

Insertion point: A short vertical line that marks the location where text you type will appear.

Justified paragraph alignment: The left and right edges of each line are aligned with the margin.

Landscape orientation: Lines of text are parallel to the paper's long edge.

Leader character: A character, such as a hyphen, that fills the tab space between words.

Left paragraph alignment: The left edge of each line is even with the left margin.

Left tab: The left edge of text aligns at the tab stop.

Macro: A group of commands to execute, bundled together under one name. Rather than running each command separately, you just run the macro and it in turn runs all the commands automatically.

Match Case: Word matches upper- and lowercase letters in a Find operation. For example, "Sales" will not match "sales" or "SALES."

Move: To move a section of text from one location to another. You end up with one copy of the text in the new location.

Point: A measurement of character size and spacing. One point is 1/72 of an inch.

Portrait orientation: Lines of text are parallel to the paper's short edge.

Right paragraph alignment: The right edge of each line is even with the right margin.

Right tab: The right edge of text aligns at the tab stop.

Selection bar: The part of the screen to the left of the text. Can be used with the mouse to select text.

Shortcut key: A key, or combination of keys, you can use to issue a command without using the menus.

Strikethrough: A character style that makes the text look as if it were crossed out.

Style: A collection of specifications for formatting text (for example 12-point centered Courier text). A style may include information for the font, size, style, margins, and spacing. Applying a style to text automatically formats the text according to that style's specifications.

Whole Words Only: Only whole words will be found in a Find operation. For example, if you are searching for "and" Word will not consider "band" to be a match.

Wrapping: Automatically starting a new line when you reach the right margin.

Index

135

136

V

vertical
     line on-screen (insertion point), 28
     orientation (portrait), 91-92, 130
View menu commands
     bullets beside, 105
     Draft, 107
     Normal, 105
     Outline, 105
     Page Layout, 105
     Ribbon, 72
     Ruler, 46, 87

W-Z

whole words only, searching for, 53, 130
WIN command, 12
Windows, starting, 12
Word
     exiting, 26
     features, 1
     installing, 127-128
     screen components, 2, 15
     starting, 13-14
Word icon, 13
WordPerfect Help (Help menu) command, 20
words, selecting, 41
workspace, blank, 69
wrapping text, 28, 130